The North Norfolk Coast

John Carter (Bean's Seal Trips) and Paul Bishop (Bishop's Boats) selling tickets for their trips to observe the seal colony and birdlife at Blakeney Point, April 2001. Such trips have been organized by these companies since shortly after the Second World War. Today boats set out from Blakeney Harbour and Morston Quay seven days a week between the months of April and October, weather permitting. It is always a fascinating excursion, but warm clothing and waterproofs are advisable! (*Author's collection*)

BRITAIN IN OLD PHOTOGRAPHS

The North Norfolk Coast

NEIL R. STOREY

SUTTON PUBLISHING

Sutton Publishing Limited
Phoenix Mill · Thrupp · Stroud
Gloucestershire · GL5 2BU

First published 2001

Copyright © Neil R. Storey, 2001

Cover photographs:
Half title photograph: Sheringham Shannock
brothers and lifeboatmen Henry 'Joyful'
West BEM and Jack West. (*Author's
collection*)
Title page: Sarah and Karen Hall in the
horseshoe pool on Cromer beach, 1976.
(*Author's collection*)

British Library Cataloguing in Publication Data
A catalogue record for this book is available from the
British Library.

ISBN 0-7509-2825 5

Typeset in 10.5/13.5 Photina.
Typesetting and origination by
Sutton Publishing Limited.
Printed and bound in England by
J.H. Haynes & Co. Ltd, Sparkford.

This book is dedicated to Sarah and Miles.

The beach, Bacton-on-Sea, *c.* 1910.

CONTENTS

Fishing boats on Cromer beach, 2001. (*Author's collection*)

INTRODUCTION

For people of quiet yet deep native pride and warmth; for history so diverse and yet still shaped and dominated by the sea; for flora and fauna which may be observed in its own natural habitat; for contrasting landscape, from high cliffs and mellow hills to salt marsh and sandy marrams, there really is nowhere *quite* like North Norfolk. This place is loved by all who know it well; truly, it is one of the most precious gems of this sceptred isle.

North Norfolk folk are different: they have always worked hard to fish and farm here. The same sea which enriches our air, shimmers with sun-catching waves in the summer and yields so much to our fishermen, can take lives in the turn of a wind or the crash of a wave. The same sea that has carried sand bars and spits to silt up once prosperous medieval ports like Brancaster, Holme, Blakeney and Cley has all but swallowed settlements and towns like Shipden, Eccles, Keswick and Whimpwell.

Strictly speaking, the classic North Norfolk coastal settlements were those near Wells and along the coast to centre around Cromer and just beyond to Mundesley. Most of them are encompassed in this

Four children and their boat with an improvised mast and sail at Blakeney, *c.* 1912. (*Author's collection*)

old rhyme, which reflects local legends and nicknames in its rhyming couplets. Doddermen is a Norfolk word for snails:

Cromer crabs,
Runton dabs;
Beeston babies,
Sheringham ladies;
Weybourne witches,
Cley bitches,
Salthouse ditches;
Langham fairmaids,
Blakeney bulldogs;

Morston doddermen,
Binham bulls,
Stiffkey blues,
Wells bitefingers,
And the Blakeney people
Stand on the Steeple,
And crack hazel-nuts
With a five-farthing beetle.

This book, however, encompasses all points on the northern coast of Norfolk from Hunstanton to Winterton in the form of an unashamedly nostalgic and meandering journey along the old coast road now known as the A149 as far as Cromer where we join the B1159 for our final destination. Of course, as any good guide to our beloved North Norfolk would, I will be stopping off at towns and villages for a bit of a look around. On our explorations I hope to renew memories of views, streets trades and businesses once taken as 'part of the fixtures' which have changed dramatically or have simply disappeared with time and tide over the last 100 years. I also wish to introduce some of my favourite characters and images from the past; they may not be as famous as Nelson or Coxswain Blogg, but they are still indicative of North Norfolk.

Until the nineteenth century the North Norfolk coast was made up of small communities which made a living almost entirely from fishing, farming and sea trading. Its waters were known and feared for their long, sad story of shipwreck, disaster and loss of life; not surprisingly the mariners of old bestowed the title of 'The Devil's Throat' upon it. Today it is almost impossible to think that until the nineteenth century there was no great vogue for seaside holidays. The only visitors were those rich enough to come and 'take the waters' and enjoy the fresh sea air for predominantly medical reasons.

As the Victorians' passion for 'fresh air therapy' grew and the railways came to Norfolk from the mid nineteenth century, many coastal villages became towns and resorts. As the popularity of the towns grew, the writings of Clement Scott in his 'Poppyland' stories published in the *Daily Telegraph* in the 1880s fuelled the public's imagination and desire to visit this wonderfully picturesque place. Trains began to run direct from London Liverpool Street to North Walsham and Cromer. The journey to Cromer was eventually achieved in 175 minutes by 'The Norfolk Coast Express' – the pride of the Great Eastern Railway. Grand hotels with full liveried staff were built for the large numbers of visiting gentlefolk; promenades, piers and boulevards were constructed. The rest, as we shall see, is history.

Our journey along the North Norfolk Coast, with just a few diversions along the way, covers about 50 miles of coastal road and byways familiar to anyone who knows and loves this very special area. Here the roadways are still gently dusted with windblown sand; clusters of scarlet sun-kissed poppies fill the waysides, along with a cornucopia of wild flowers and plants which sway and bob while pied wagtails sweep and dive out of hedgerows as cars pass by.

This is a coastline of changes and contrasts. We begin our journey at New Hunstanton, a town built specifically as a seaside resort by Henry Styleman le Strange in the middle of the nineteenth century. Here the extensive green sweeps down to the esplanade. From this fine vantage point the phenomenon of the sun apparently setting over the sea instead of over land may be observed. New Hunstanton has the unique distinction of being the only resort on the east coast to face west. We proceed up the gradual incline as the cliffs rise to over 60ft and begin our journey in earnest at Old Hunstanton. Here was the ancestral home of the le Stranges, Lords of the Manor and hereditary Lord High Admirals of the Wash. According to this last title le Strange was entitled to everything in the Wash as far as a man

A huge crowd complete with banners gather for a religious 'camp' meeting on the beach at Sheringham, *c.* 1908. (*Author's collection*)

on horseback could throw a javelin at low tide. Story has it that in the 1930s this right was exercised when Mercedes Gleitze, the German long-distance swimmer, swam the Wash. Once ashore she was claimed as the legal property of the le Stranges! At least temporarily so.

Onward through the open marshland rich in birdlife to the charming villages of Holme-next-the-Sea, Thornham and Titchwell, to Brancaster and Brancaster Staithe, known as Branodunum to the Romans who established a fortified outpost of their empire here.

Next come the Burnhams; an attractive group of seven parishes, they now include Burnham Deepdale, Norton, Overy, Sutton, Ulph and Westgate (or Market). The group originally included the parishes of St Andrew and St Edmund, but these were absorbed by Westgate and Overy respectively and the more distant Deepdale and Thorpe have taken their place.

As the coastline becomes obscured by lines of Corsica pines, it is soon clear you are at Holkham; these trees mark the border between land and sand just about all the way to Wells. The landscape then opens up, revealing broad skies over salt marshes and muddy estuaries of outstanding national importance for wildlife and nature. Travelling through this area you cross little hump-backed bridges over streams, skirting marshes and villages where the buildings are a distinctive blend of Norfolk red brick, flints and beach pebbles.

The country changes here to become quite hilly between Holt and Cromer, this area being denoted on old maps as the East Anglian Heights. Here trees canopy the inland roads at Upper Sheringham through to Holt, while bracken, bright yellow gorse and heather carpet the landscape.

At Weybourne and on to Sheringham the hills allow the traveller to observe the land laid out before him as if on a map. Gone is the coastal marshland; here the land rises to high cliffs where the

Fishermen's memorial chapel, Winterton, c. 1932.

fields terminate at edges made jagged by the erosion and landfall over the years. This area, extending to Cromer, Sidestrand and on to Mundesley, is classic North Norfolk.

Along the coast from Cromer at Trimingham the cliffs and hills rise to some of the highest points in Norfolk. Since the Second World War the military has had a strong presence here with a radar station; today it decorates the landscape with a great white 'golf ball' which is visible for miles around.

Beyond 'Poppyland' the seaside settlements become less touched by tourist amenities until we reach the delightfully unspoilt village of Happisburgh, famed for its red-and-white-hooped lighthouse. Here the soil is very good and holidaymakers have the unusual experience of witnessing a fine harvest gathered in on the fields by the cliff's edge.

South from Happisburgh the cliffs gradually decline into sandy dunes with a generous covering of marram grass. Here the land is very flat and large tracts have been lost by encroachments of sea and erosion over the years. Today Eccles comprises just a few scattered houses. It was once a town and port spread over 2,000 acres, but after a tremendous sea surge on 4 January 1604 it was claimed that barely 100 acres were left. Another more recent example of the sea's awesome power may be found in the neighbouring village of Sea Palling, where most of the houses on the seaward side of the settlement were wiped out or terribly damaged in the 1953 floods. It is estimated that along the entire North Norfolk coastline erosion is occuring at a rate of 1 to 5 yards a year.

At Horsey the land faces a double jeopardy as this narrow neck of coast is bordered by broad and sea with only 1 mile of marsh to separate them. Liable to flooding, it suffered in the 1953 deluge along with the rest of the coast. The worst breach, however, came in February 1938 when 15 square miles were flooded after severe storms. Today Horsey offers a fine mooring for Broads visitors. Behind its restored drainage mill may be seen the modern electricity generating windmills of West Somerton, a curious yet somehow inoffensive feature of the modern Norfolk coastline. Another Norfolk giant came from this tiny village; Robert Hales (1820–63) was claimed to be the biggest man in the western world at the time, standing 7ft 6in.

We complete our journey at Winterton. In the seventeenth century Winterton Ness, 'the most infamous spot between Tyne and Thames', was a promontory which swept outwards from the shore and lay in wait to catch any vessel which failed to give it a sufficiently wide berth. Today this great danger has been scoured away by the sea but its legacy lives on in Winterton village which was, according to local lore, founded on the timbers of wrecks. Daniel Defoe, author and traveller, wrote of it in 1722: 'There was not a shed, nor a barn, nor a stable, nay not the pale of their fences and yards, not a hogstye but what was made of planks, beams, wales and timbers, the wreck of ships and the ruin of merchants and mariners fortunes.'

Clement Scott lived to regret his promotion of his beloved 'Poppyland', often wishing he had kept it to himself to prevent it from becoming 'bungalow land'. Those who can remember the fields swaying with crimson poppies are getting fewer by the year; their beauty, dignity and innocence was something which belonged to a world before two world wars. Fortunately there is still so much beauty here, so much peace – best we all treasure it.

Neil R. Storey
North Walsham, 2001

1

Hunstanton to the Burnhams

A typical multi-view greetings card sent from Hunstanton by holidaymakers in the 1950s.
(*Author's collection*)

The Green, Hunstanton, *c.* 1925. To the left of centre is the Golden Lion Hotel. Opened in 1846 as The New Inn, this was the first building constructed in Henry Styleman le Strange's planned holiday resort of New Hunstanton. At this stage in the development it was the only building standing between Hunstanton Lighthouse and Heacham. Effectively in the middle of nowhere, it attracted the critical nickname of 'le Strange's folly'. (*Author's collection*)

The cross and the pier, Hunstanton, *c.* 1910. This shaft of a cross was placed on the stepped plinth specially constructed for it shortly after the first buildings were erected around the Green. Uncertainty surrounds its origins. The most plausible theory is that it is part of the village cross brought from Snettisham to Old Hunstanton by members of the le Strange family when they inherited their title and estates. Reaching 800 yards out to sea is Hunstanton Pier built in 1870 for £2,000. The pier was hit by a number of disasters, the most serious being a fire that almost destroyed the pavilion. After the Second World War the pier gradually became dilapidated. Badly damaged by storms, the last remaining remnants were blown up on local authority orders in 1979. (*Author's collection*)

Parasols and dresses for ladies, gents in sports jackets, baggy trousers, belts and braces along the beach and promenade in high summer at New Hunstanton, *c.* 1935. (*Author's collection*)

The open-air bathing pool, South Promenade, Hunstanton, *c.* 1937. It was opened in 1928 on land reclaimed by the construction of the sea wall between 1924 and 1928. This sea wall was extended south in 1931–2 at a cost of £20,000 and a boating lake with an island, ornamental gardens and shelters were constructed over the reclaimed land. Most of this has disappeared today; the 4-acre site is now occupied by car parks and caravan sites. (*Author's collection*)

The distinctive golden browns and muddy yellows of the locally hewn carrstone of the shop frontages contrast with the white pull-down shutters along New Hunstanton High Street, *c.* 1930. Along its length in the 1930s every necessity and most luxuries could be obtained. Among the shops seen here are on the right, Christopher William Abbs, tobacconist, in The Corner House, Walter Henry Lenton's chemists, J.T. Whomes, bakers, and on the left numbers 10, 13 and 15 are occupied by Walton Bros, outfitters. (*Author's collection*)

On the beach, Hunstanton, *c.* 1905. Behind the seaside revellers one of the North Norfolk coast's most unusual geographic features may be seen – the strata that make up the high cliffs. The base is carrstone of dark brown tint below and yellow above. On this rests a band of bright red chalk, above which, forming the top of the cliff, is white chalk. (*Author's collection*)

The ruins of St Edmund's shrine and the lighthouse, Hunstanton, *c.* 1930. Here, at the cliffs' highest point (65ft) stand the ruins of a fifteenth-century chapel built in honour of St Edmund. Local tradition states he landed here after his travels in Germany to be crowned King of East Anglia. In the background is the lighthouse built by Trinity House in the 1830s; it ceased operating in 1921. It was restored to become a holiday home in the 1960s. (*Author's collection*)

A well-attended and strictly observed feature of the Hunstanton maritime calendar was its regatta. Here the yachts approach the marker buoy in the Prince of Wales Cup Race, July 1947. (*Author's collection*)

The cliffs and beach, Old Hunstanton, *c. 1935*. Here the cliffs smooth down into dunes. This view shows us much of the most westerly part of the North Norfolk coastline. (*Author's collection*)

Old Hunstanton village, *c. 1933*. This view greeted the traveller leaving New Hunstanton on the coast road on the first leg of the journey along the northern coastline of Norfolk. It is still easily recognizable today. (*Author's collection*)

A frequently captured view often entitled 'A Quaint Corner of Old Hunstanton' on old postcards and in illustrated guidebooks of the early twentieth century. This view of Church Street dates from the early 1950s. The church, dedicated to St Mary the Virgin, has been twice restored by members of the le Strange family: Sir Hamon in the fourteenth century and Sir Henry in the mid-nineteenth century. (*Author's collection*)

Hunstanton Hall and gatehouse, Old Hunstanton, *c.* 1935. A manor in the hands of the le Strange family stood here from the fourteenth century. Rebuilt in the late fifteenth century by Sir Roger, it was further added to and developed by his son and nephew. Best remembered of all the family, however, is the Sir Roger le Strange born at the hall in 1616, not for his inept attempt to recapture King's Lynn from the Parliamentary forces during the English Civil War; not for his being in charge of all the printing machines of England after the restoration, nor his voracious pamphleteering; but for his gift to literature of the first translation of Aesop's *Fables* into English. Little of the magnificent hall stands today following disastrous fires in 1853 and 1958. The le Stranges, stalwarts of the local community for 800 years, had already been pushed out of their ancestral home in 1948 when heavy taxation forced them to sell. (*Author's collection*)

Village Street, Holme-next-the-Sea, *c.* 1935. The unmetalled road, neat verges and five-bar gate complete the rura image. The church tower of St Mary the Virgin is on the right. It was raised and the chancel rebuilt by Henry (Nottingham during the reign of Henry IV. (*Author's collection*)

Beach Road, Holme-next-the-Sea, *c.* 1935. Near here is one end of the Peddar's Way, the Roman road that course across the county and into Suffolk giving the legions access to the tribal areas of the Iceni. Holme was probab the landing point for ferries that crossed the Wash from Lincolnshire, bringing troops of the Ninth Legion who ha been summoned by the signal of the beacon at Thornham. (*Author's collection*)

Whitehall Farm and camp site, Holme-next-the-Sea, *c.* 1923. The farm was kept at the time by Frederick Hiam who went on to become Sir Frederick, one of the chief landowners in the area. The land around the village was very productive. Crops grown here included wheat, barley, turnips, beans and mangold wurzel. (*Author's collection*)

The sand dunes, Holme-next-the-Sea, *c.* 1935. This area is one of outstanding natural beauty, covering 224 acres of grass-carpeted dunes. It was given by the Norfolk Naturalists Trust to the National Trust in 1967. (*Author's collection*)

A ring of sand bags surrounds the Bronze Age timber circle dubbed 'Sea' or 'Wood' Henge at Holme-next-the-Sea. In 1998 field work was begun by the Norfolk Archaeological Unit on the recently exposed ring. In January 1999 a national newspaper put the site on its cover and massive public interest ensued as hundreds flocked to visit it. As spring passed into summer the interest did not abate. The eliptical ring of fifty-five close-set oak timbers was dated to about 2000 BC. It was proposed that the ancient timbers be removed to the specialist conservation centre at Flag Fen. This was carried out but not without provoking protests from some locals and interested parties, including druids. The circle has been removed and conserved; there has even been a Channel 4 *Time Team Special* programme reconstructing how and why it was built. Debate still goes on over where it will finally be displayed or if it should be reburied. (*Eastern Counties Newspapers*)

Thornham Street, *c.* 1910. This delightful view, taken when the village was colloquially known as 'Rosy Thornham', has changed little in ninety years. However, the road has been metalled, the trunk of tree on the right now fills the rails which surround it and a village sign adorns the green. (*Author's collection*)

King's Head, Thornham, 1951. Here a leaded window bore the scratched message 'J. Horne put me here and bid me stand for many a year. 1771'. The pub sign, along with a number of still extant wrought-iron features in the village and church, are the few reminders left of the Thornham iron works founded by Mrs Edith Ames-Lyde in the 1880s as a source of employment for local men. This project came to a sad end after her death in 1914 and many men being taken for service in the First World War. The works closed in July 1920. (*Author's collection*)

The Chequers Commercial Inn, Thornham, 1941. Dating from the early nineteenth century, the Chequers was probably built to meet the anticipated increased demands of the coaching traffic passing along the new road cut through the centre of the village and through the gardens of the Red House and the Cottage. (*Author's collection*)

The Three Horse Shoes, Titchwell, 1939. In the mid-nineteenth century this pub was kept by John Temple. It was one of just three non-farming businesses in the village, the others being Robert Oake the shoemaker and the village shop kept by John Youngs whose descendants ran it well into the twentieth century. The population of Titchwell has remained constant over the last 150 years – about 150 souls. (*Author's collection*)

The keepers' hut at the bird sanctuary, Scolt Head, Brancaster, *c.* 1935. Access when this picture was taken was by boat, as it still is today. This island is internationally renowned for its nesting colony of Sandwich terns and large numbers of migratory birds. It was preserved for the future by the visionary work of Professor F.W. Oliver and Dr S.H. Long. The site is now in the shared care of the National Trust and the Norfolk Naturalists Trust. (*Author's collection*)

e Street, Brancaster, *c.* 1930. On the right is the Ship Hotel, a village pub since 1747. In its time it has acted as temporary mortuary and hospital for shipwrecked sailors. In the closing years of the eighteenth century and rly nineteenth century Admiral Nelson visited a number of times to call on his nanny whose son ran the pub. e Ship's end wall is adorned with a large model ship of the line from the Nelson period. The model is thought to in excess of 100 years old and has hung in the pub for fifty years. Today, after passing through a number of nds, the Ship enjoys a bright future under the energetic management of Mike and Ali Chesterman. (*Author's llection*)

The Gap, Brancaster, *c.* 1948. Near here is the site of the fort and early dwellings of the Roman town
Branodunum. Established here in about AD 230, the fort garrisoned troops to guard this territory against possib
invasion by Saxon marauders. Today this area of firm beach, sandy dunes and reclaimed marsh is mostly und
the care of the National Trust which established a field study centre at Dial House, Brancaster Staithe, in 199
On the left is the club house of the Royal West Norfolk Golf Club, formed in 1892. Its links, laid out over th
common, is still regarded as one of the finest in the country. (*Author's collection*)

fine study of the harbour, Brancaster Staithe, *c.* 1925. In the mid-1920s there were about fourteen whelk boats Brancaster Staithe. The fishermen were listed in *Kelly's Norfolk Directory* as Herbert Winterbourne; Ernest, ₃nry, Henry (junr.), Thomas and William Loose (who was also coxswain of the lifeboat); John, Richard and illiam Southerland. To the right is the wooden coastguard lookout tower moved from Scolt Head to the harbour 1908. Originally it was only manned in stormy weather but a third storey was added in the 1930s and a ₃rmanent watch staff stationed there throughout the Second World War. It was sold as a holiday home in 1949 ₃d has remained in the same family's hands ever since. (*Author's collection*)

₃posite: High water at the Harbour, Brancaster Staithe, *c.* 1925. At this time whelks were the predominant catch the fishermen. All the buildings on the right were whelk houses where the shellfish were washed, boiled and ₃pared for sale. A familiar sight then were the younger sons of fishing families who would hop on their bikes to ₃t as 'hawkers', marketing the catch to the more affluent houses and hotels to the west of the village. (*Author's 'lection*)

The Market Place looking west, Burnham Market, *c.* 1910. How this wide open plain has changed! The view has, in fact, become greener. The butcher's shop, centre right, has been demolished and the greens on the right have been planted with trees which are today reaching full, leafy maturity. The wide, compacted grit market place once renowned for its provision market and holiday fairs has been reduced to a road which, along with the little stream known as Goose Beck, snakes through the village. (*Author's collection*)

wer Market Place and North Street junction, Burnham Market, *c.* 1925. On the left are members of the Gollege mily who ran the tobacconist for many years. Next door is Daniel Searle's drapers and outfitters while on e right is Barclays Bank. In the 1920s Burnham Market was firmly established as the chief town among all the urnhams. By the Burnham Market Order of 1928 the parishes of Burnham Ulph and Sutton and Burnham estgate were united to form the parish of Burnham Market. This new parish consisted of 4,551 acres with a pulation of 1,131. (*Author's collection*)

posite: The Rose & Crown, Burnham Market, 1939, kept at the time by John Robert Bickell. Situated on the rth side of the Market Place at the bottom of Herring's Lane, it closed in the late 1960s. (*Author's collection*)

East end of Market Place and Front Street, Burnham Market, *c.* 1948. On the right is G.W. Roy's fancy repository and the post office. Just beyond that is the Black Horse pub, run throughout the nineteenth century (when it was know as the Wild Horse) by the Habberton family who also owned a saddlers and harness-makers beside the pub until the 1920. (*Author's collection*)

Burnham Market war memorial on the green at the south side of the Market Place, *c.* 1948. It was unveiled in the 1920s by Lord Leicester; the Revd T.F. Faulkner conducted the service. (*Author's collection*)

e Hoste Arms Hotel, Burnham Market, *c.* 1950. Originally built as the manor house of Burnham Westgate in
30, it was later opened as a coaching inn by the Pitt family. It has a chequered past having been a court house
the local assizes, an auction house and a brothel. Lord Nelson called to collect his dispatches here – what
nction the building was fulfilling at the time we can but speculate! Sadly the Hoste Arms suffered about a
ntury of architectural abuse and neglect under brewery ownership until it was purchased in 1989 by Paul
hittome, a man who has loved the North Norfolk coast since childhood. For Mr Whittome, owning the Hoste
as a confessed dream come true and what a hotel he has made it. It was voted by *The Times* as the second
ourite hotel in England and twenty-seventh favourite in the world. (*Author's collection*)

Burnham Market market place, *c.* 1948. The quiet little place of the 1930s became a bustling country town aft
the Second World War. Although it still retains its character and charm, along with banks and butchers, there a
now also art galleries, craft centres and antiquarian bookshops. It also reflects a sad trend in North Norfolk:
many people move to the area from other counties, especially in retirement or to buy a holiday retreat, that loc
young folk whose families have lived here for many years cannot afford to buy a home. The trend has been
strong in this village that Burnham is nicknamed 'Little London'. (*Author's collection*)

rnham Overy Staithe, *c.* 1935. Here the River Burn runs out to sea and its creek winds out from the harbour
tween lavender-covered salt marshes. It then emerges out into the sea between sand dunes which stretch away
Holkham in the east and Scolt Head to the west. (*Author's collection*)

posite: High tide at Burnham Overy Staithe, *c.* 1950. Centre right is the Hard, which fills up with cars in the
mmer months. Many come just to enjoy the surroundings but most visit the creek for the sailing. Little has
anged today although the traditional white sails have been joined by the garish colours of windsurfers. (*Author's
lection*)

Packing mussels at Burnham Overy Staithe, *c.* 1948. This is the last business left of the sea trade that bustled in this harbour up to the mid-nineteenth century. Considerable trade was carried out in coal, corn and oysters. In 1845, when William Cringle was the Master Mariner, it was recorded that fifteen fishermen and five boats were regularly employed here. By the time this photograph was taken a mere handful of hardy men harvested mussels. (*Author's collection*)

The Moorings hotel, Burnham Overy, *c.* 1935. Sadly no longer a hotel, The Moorings always had the reputation for buying the best of the catch from the local fishermen. One contemporary account lists a 'fairly good catch' from one fishing expedition which included a few butts or dabs, small bass, grey mullet, codling, perch and herring, eighty 'phosphorescent mackrel', a score of trout, one of which was 'a glorious nine pounder (The Moorings Hotel snapped him up)'. (*Author's collection*)

The Hard by Burnham Overy Staithe, *c.* 1948. It is out of season and the scene is very tranquil – you can almost taste the fresh sea air in this evocative photograph, feel the cool breeze, watch the rabbit-filled sand hills and hear the clicking of the shrouds against the masts, along with the warbles and calls of the wealth of birdlife here. (*Author's collection*)

Post office corner, Burnham Overy Staithe, *c.* 1948. Begun as a village store at the end of the nineteenth century, it became a sub-post office in the 1900s and was kept well into the twentieth century by generations of the Riches family. When James Vincent Riches was sub-postmaster in the early 1930s the first public telephone in the village was installed here. Previously the nearest money order and telegraph office was 2 miles distant at Burnham Market. (*Author's collection*)

Creek Road, Burnham Overy Staithe, *c.* 1948. Here is the unmistakable entrance road to the Staithe. It has hard changed today. (*Author's collection*)

.urnham Overy windmill, *c.* 1910. The mill is still a familiar landmark beside the A149 coast road. It was built in 816 by Edmund Savory to supplement the work of his water mill at the bottom of the hill. It remained in the mily's hands until John Savory sold it to Sidney Dewing in 1900 who in turn sold it to Sidney Everitt, a maltster om Wells, in 1910. Falling into disrepair by the time of the First World War, it ceased working in 1919. Its .ternal machinery was removed and its shell sold in 1926 to Mr H.C. Hughes of Grantchester who converted it .to a holiday residence. In 1957 it was restored and a year later was given by Mr Hughes to the National Trust . whose hands it remains today. It is leased out as a private residence. (*Author's collection*)

pposite: The village street, Burnham Overy Staithe, *c.* 1937. On the main coast road on the right is the Hero .ıblic house kept at the time by Charles Harold Bangham. The pub was named in honour of the county's, and .guably the country's, greatest maritime hero, Admiral Lord Nelson, who was born just a few miles away at .ırnham Thorpe. It is interesting to note that in 1937 there were sixteen pubs in *Kelly's Norfolk Directory* named . honour of the the great admiral. (*Author's collection*)

Savory's Mill, Burnham Overy, *c.* 1910. Built in 1767 it remained in the Savory family's hands throughout th nineteenth century until it was sold along with the post mill to Sidney Dewing in 1900. The watermill was so again in 1910 to Sidney Everitt who retained it when he sold the tower windmill. Worked until after the Secor World War, the watermill was gutted by fire in 1959. Carefully rebuilt, it is now in the care of the National Tru and leased out as a private residence. (*Author's collection*)

Opposite: The Avenue, Burnham Overy, *c.* 1919. In the distance Savory's watermill can just be seen. T unmetalled road surface made up of Wymondham flints and binding silt harks back to a lost age of horse-drav transport which caused the cart tracks in the roadway. It is all a far cry from the busy main coastal road we knc today. (*Author's collection*)

The cottages by Mill Corner at Burnham Overy, *c.* 1935. In the careful composition of this image the photographer has instructed the residents of the cottages to stand in front of their doorways – something they no doubt willingly complied with for the honour and novelty of being in a photograph. It was once a familiar feature here for washing to be hung out along the fences of the front gardens. With the traffic which passes through in the summer today washing would turn grey rather than white as it dried! (*Author's collection*)

NELSON 1801.

Admiral Lord Horatio Nelson (1758–1805), Norfolk's – and arguably the nation's – greatest maritime hero. Born the son of Edmund, Rector of Burnham Thorpe, he was educated at Downham Market, Norwich, and the Paston School, North Walsham. From there he left to take up his first position in the Royal Navy at the age of twelve. Volumes have been written on his noble and brave exploits. A brilliant tactician, his most notable victories were at the Nile in 1798; Copenhagen in 1801; and Trafalgar in 1805 where he was mortally wounded and died just as victory was declared. There are many reminders of the great admiral in the county; many civic buildings are dedicated to him. Nelson was a man of the people, inspiring yet humane. He is a hero for all ages and his name is known to every Norfolkman true of heart to this day. Nelson said on his return to his native county after his victory at the Nile: 'I am myself a Norfolk man, and glory in being so.' (*Author's collection*)

urnham Thorpe Rectory in which Horatio Nelson was born on 29 September 1758. Sadly this building was ulled down after his father's death in 1802 and replaced by the one which stands today. (*Author's collection*)

ie Creek, Burnham Thorpe, *c.* 1905. Here the young Horatio Nelson sailed his toy boats. At the Creek and on sits to Burnham Overy Staithe and Wells his fascination with sailing and the sea was kindled. (*Author's collection*)

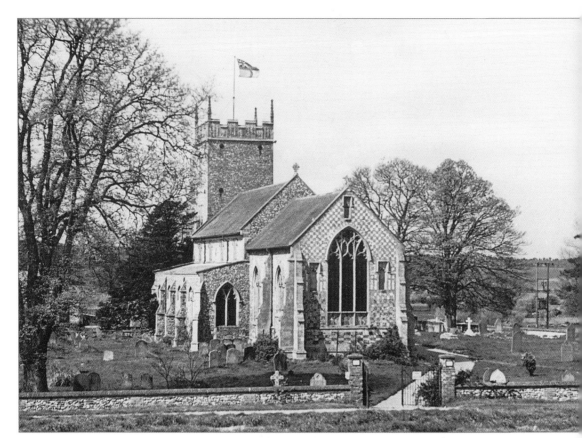

All Saints' Church, Burnham Thorpe, *c.* 1955. The church is flying the pre-1801 white ensign, the naval flag Nelson would have been most familiar with. This is an honour which was granted to this church by the Admiralty in the 1920s to mark the village's connection with the maritime hero. Inside are memorials to other members of the Nelson family and the great admiral, including timbers from HMS *Victory* made into church furniture and a magnificent bust of Nelson presented by the London Society of East Anglians. (*Author's collection*)

2

Holkham to Salthouse

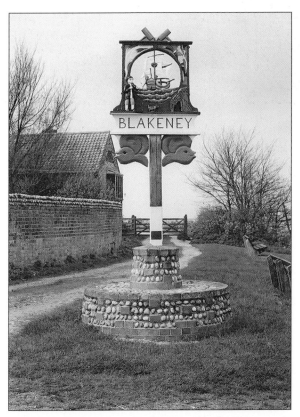

Blakeney village sign presented by the local Women's Institute to commemorate their golden jubilee year in 1965. (*Author's collection*)

Holkham Hall and Country Fair, July 1999. Begun by Thomas Coke between 1734 and 1760 Holkham Hall is one of the finest Palladian mansions in the country. Built on the wealth of agriculture the great house eventually passed to Thomas's great-nephew, Thomas William Coke, who is still recognized as one of the nation's great agricultural reformers and improvers. Among his achievements was the introduction of the 'Holkham Shearings' – a forerunner of modern agricultural shows. (*Author's collection*)

'Throwing a jug'. Cyril Ruffles at work at the potter's wheel, Holkham Pottery, *c.* 1955. Cyril began his working life at the nearby Peterstone brickyard where his father was foreman. When Lady Leicester began the pottery in 1951 she brought Cyril to work there to create a range of pottery to sell during open days at Holkham Hall. (*Author's collection*)

Holkham Dunes, part of Holkham Meals, 2001. These dunes were planted with Corsica pines by Thomas William Coke in the mid-nineteenth century. His intention was to stabilize the sand to enable the land behind to be reclaimed from the sea. Today this area of outstanding natural beauty is England's largest designated National Nature Reserve. Covering over 10,000 acres it spans over 9 miles between Burnham Overy and Blakeney and is a breeding ground for birds such as terns, oystercatchers and redshank, while in the winter it is a refuge for the likes of snow bunting, turnstone and golden plover. (*Author's collection*)

Springtime on Holkham Bay beach, 2001. The lack of cliffs, the pine-lined dunes, the great expanse of firm, wide sandy plains and the unspoilt natural beauty make this beach unique along the North Norfolk coast. The setting for many shoots for television and film, this beach was used for the final scene of the acclaimed John Madden film *Shakespeare in Love*, which starred Gwyneth Paltrow and was released in 1998. (*Author's collection*)

In the opening months of 2001 foot-and-mouth disease affected the countryside across Great Britain. To avoid the spread of the epidemic, residents in country areas visited by the public took the precaution of setting up improvised disinfectant footbaths at points of access to agricultural land. Many public footpaths were closed and warning signs like this one at Holkham were put on clear display. (*Author's collection*)

The Beach House, stables and swing boats at the top of Beach Road, Wells, *c.* 1908. For those not wishing to walk the length of Wells' grassy embankment, carts were ready to transport visitors along the mile of beach road between quay and seaside. Today many folks simply drive to the car park or enjoy the miniature steam railway. The locomotive's merry whistle may be heard across the town during the summer months. (*Author's collection*)

View from the embankment at the top of Beach Road, Wells, *c.* 1935. Before most families had their own car, coach outings and 'works beanos' were popular entertainment during the summer months. Wells was always a popular destination, and this is clear from the number of coaches in the parking area. (*Norfolk Local Studies Library*)

Abraham's Busom, *c.* 1955. This area was once one of the channels of Wells harbour but was isolated from tidal waters when the embankment was built between 1854 and 1859. This beautiful spot was covered with pine trees planted by the Earl of Leicester who leased the whole area to Wells Urban District Council for an annual sum of £10 in 1935. The caravan park in the background occupies the site of yet more forest which was wiped out by the tidal breach during the east coast floods of 1953. (*Author's collection*)

Wells life boat crew, 23 August 1905. Dressed in their official-issue cork lifebelts, they stand in front of the lifeboat house and slipway, constructed at the seaward end of the beach road in 1895 at a cost of £550. Their rescue vessel was the RNLI boat *Baltic* which served Wells between 1895 and 1913. (*Author's collection*)

The Wells motor lifeboat *Royal Silver Jubilee 1910–1935*. Pictured shortly after it was sent to the station, it served Wells between 1936 and 1945. This new craft was a great improvement on the old boat which was powered by oars and sail; it was propelled by powerful Hotchkiss Cone engines which worked on the principle of water jet propulsion. (*Author's collection*)

The new inshore rescue craft and boathouse at Wells, March 1966. On the right is the Wells lifeboat coxswain, David Cox, who is joined by crew member Mr A. Warner. (*Eastern Counties Newspapers*)

Drawing great crowds of onlookers and revellers, boats gaily decked out with signal flags and red ensigns complete the scene at the Wells Regatta in July 1925. (*Norfolk Local Studies Library*)

Staith Street, Wells, *c.* 1920. This was and still is the town's main shopping street off the quayside. All the domestic goods required by townsfolk could be purchased here. In the 1920s businesses along its length included Wells & Son drapers, Walter Chapman's chemist, International Tea Stores grocers, H.H. Harrell and Drake's butchers, James Cooper the baker, Miss Martha Loynes and Eliza Stroughhair's Fancy Repositories and George Grummett saddler, harness- and truss-maker. (*Author's collection*)

The grain ship *Zeus* loads up her cargo from Wells quayside, *c.* 1950. The distinctive granary and its gantry, which extends over the quayside, were built for F. & G. Smith, maltsters in 1906. The building has become a landmark which defines this view unmistakably as Wells. In the distance is the gable end of the old Bullard's pub the Shipwright's Arms. (*Author's collection*)

Cold winter work, December 1938. Robert Cooper, one of the oldest fishermen in Wells and one of the first Sheringham whelkers to settle there, sorts and prepares a consignment of mussels for market. (*Author's collection*)

Harvesting mussels, *c.* 1953. The mussels were sown early the previous year on the bed of the harbour at Wells. The harvesters are, left to right: Billy Platten, Derek Lack, Tony Jordan and Jimmy Shrum. Once harvested and sorted the mussels were sent on to Wales for bottling. (*Eastern Counties Newspapers*)

Bungalows, Morston, *c.* 1935. After the First World War small areas of coastal land were purchased and covered with prefabricated wooden houses and railway carriages which became holiday homes. A contemporary account recalls: 'Little wooden bungalows are not even great fun - *verb. Sap.* From one who knows. Water supply distant, sanitation primitive, cooking and lighting by paraffin oil, sand in one's food, sand pouring in at every chink when the wind blows . . . and one calls it a holiday.' (*Author's collection*)

Rather than the traditional hand sieves, workers here use machines to clean the tasty Morston mussels in 1967. Some things did remain traditional, though. Sorting was still done at the back of the machine by eye. (*Eastern Counties Newspapers*)

Stiffkey Street, complete with ox cart, *c.* 1905. This charming and sleepy coastal village is renowned the world over for its 'Stewkey Blues' (cockles) gathered beyond the marshes on High Sand, Blacknock and by the Stone Mell Creeks. The village, with its predominantly flint-faced buildings, has changed little and for most of the twentieth century its population remained below 300 souls. (*Author's collection*)

Locked out! The Revd Harold Davidson, Rector of Stiffkey and Morston for twenty-six years, is not permitted to enter his church at Stiffkey after a church court found him guilty of immoral behaviour in 1932. Proud of his title as the 'Prostitutes' Padre', he spent up to six days a week in London saving 'fallen women'. His visits were tolerated as distant good works by locals who affectionately knew him as 'Little Jimmy'. In spite of being banned from local churches he preached to large crowds on rectory lawns. Eventually he was defrocked by the Bishop of Norwich and went on fairground tours, sitting in a barrel reading from the Bible and protesting his innocence. His death was as dramatic as his life. He had a sideshow called 'A Modern Daniel in the Lion's Den', but died two days after being mauled by Freddie the lion in July 1937. (*Author's collection*)

Blakeney quayside, *c.* 1895. At this time the trading vessels which visited this little seaport for malt, grain, coal and oil-cake were becoming fewer. The spit of land at Blakeney Point was being carried farther west by tidal waters and the channel to the quayside silted up. It is now over 4 miles from the quay to the open sea. (*Author collection*)

Rebuilding and improving the Blakeney embankment which was destroyed in the 'Black Monday' tides of 29 November 1897. Maintaining the North Norfolk coast has always been a struggle against the vagaries of the sea. Embankments have been constructed here since Dutch engineers built the first such defences in this area during the seventeenth century. (*Author's collection*)

The Blakeney lifeboat *Caroline* and her crew, 1918. Unfortunately, the *Caroline*'s boathouse was on Blakeney Point and it could be forty-five minutes from the crew being alerted to the boat being launched. She was the last RNLI boat at Blakeney, serving the village from 1908 to 1935. Her worth was proved, however, with the rescue of thirty lives from two steamers on 7 and 8 January 1919, a rescue made all the more creditable when it is considered that with most of the young men of the village away at war the average age of the crew was fifty-five; seven members were over sixty. (*Author's collection*)

Blakeney High Street, *c.* 1937. On the left is the post office and general stores with a very rural Barclays Bank opposite. Further down on the left is the Ship Inn kept by Arthur Shreeve and further still the famous White Horse pub kept by Herbert Charles Long, the last coxswain of the Blakeney lifeboat. (*Norfolk Local Studies Library*)

Quay, Lower High Street and Guildhall Café, Blakeney, *c.* 1950. The café was run from the 1930s by the Misses Page. An affectionately remembered eatery, it offered a fine break from sailing for coffee, luncheons of both 'ins' and 'outs' (picnics), afternoon tea and 'sip and sup' between six and ten in the evening. (*Author's collection*)

Spring tide at Blakeney, *c.* 1935. The tide at Blakeney is peculiar. It comes in twice a day over the 4 miles of mudbanks and sand and arrives about an hour and a half after high water at the bar. On a neap tide with an unfavourable wind it may not come in at all and on a good spring tide, as seen here, it may come over the quayside right up to the Blakeney Hotel. (*Author's collection*)

Ready to go boating around the quay at Blakeney, *c.* 1955. This is no doubt a very nostalgic view for anyone who has grown up with summer holiday visits to the village. Boating is as fondly remembered as trips to Blakeney Point to see the seals, crabbing with a line off the quay using whelks bought from the local fish stall as bait and watching the sailing craft at Blakeney Regatta. Happy days. (*Author's collection*)

A charming view of Blakeney quay, 1911. No white railings guard the quayside and the old warehouses and sheds still provide the backdrop of a truly rural fishing village rarely noted by any tourist guides in 1911, except in passing references to the area being favoured by 'sporting types' for shooting fowl in the wintertime. (*Norfolk Local Studies Library*)

The *Taffy*, Page & Turner's 173-ton vessel, said to be the largest steamer ever to dock at Blakeney quay, *c.* 1905. No one event marked the end of Blakeney as a port but the death knell was certainly sounded in 1922 when Page & Turner, the last big corn merchants and mercantile traders, removed their business to offices in Holt. (*Author's collection*)

Blakeney quayside, 2001. Gone are the old buildings behind the quay, among them the Crown and the Anchor Inn, known locally as 'The Barking Dicky' because of the braying donkeys kept there. The pubs were demolished in 1921 in a scheme to clear the area for the construction of the Blakeney Hotel which was built at a cost of £31,000 in 1923 for Elsden & Co. Ltd of Holt. Elsden remained proprietors for a number of years before control reverted to the Deterding family who owned the hotel until the late twentieth century. One of the most delightful and unspoilt villages on the North Norfolk coast, Blakeney is known and loved by visitors from all over the world. No guidebook would dare omit it today. (*Author's collection*)

St Nicholas' Church, Blakeney, *c.* 1920. The rich wool merchants of Blakeney erected this magnificent building on the dilapidated structure of a smaller church in thanksgiving for their good fortune. It includes one of the finest hammer-beam roofs in Norfolk and is crowned with a 104ft tower. On the north-east corner is a distinctive narrow beacon turret from which a light shone at night to guide mariners into the harbour. (*Author's collection*)

St Mary's Church, Wiveton, and motor touring coach, *c.* 1910. This church stands proudly above the medieval bridge known locally as 'Nowhere'. In the sixteenth century Raulf Grenewey endowed the parish with a bequest of a dole which was to be regularly distributed to thirteen poor people. In a 1969 guidebook it was noted that the dole 'is still collected when the church wardens ring the bell on Saturday afternoons'. (*Author's collection*)

St Margaret's Church, Cley, *c.* 1949. Viewed across the green at Newgate at the southern end of the village and built on a slight eminence is the church of St Margaret. It is easily missed by the passing tourist, but those who seek it out are richly rewarded as it is without doubt among the most interesting and finest in this county, which has the greatest concentration of medieval churches in Europe. Built in the thirteenth century and restored and enlarged in the fourteenth, here architecture, monuments, church furniture and windows can delight and surprise even the most experienced church historian. (*Author's collection*)

Cley Mill, *c.* 1949. Erected at the turn of the nineteenth century it was worked by generations of the Burroughes family until 1921 when it was bought by Mrs S.M. Wilson for £350. She converted it into a dwelling and holiday home for her family. This mill and its unspoilt locale have probably graced more photographic film and artists' canvas than any other in the country. (*Author's collection*)

Cley street, *c. 1895*. When this photograph was taken there were plans to change this quiet village into a railway town on the Eastern & Midlands Railway with a station built near the village centre. Fortunately, this did not happen and the nearest station to Cley remained 4 miles away in Holt. (*Author's collection*)

Boats on the water near the George Inn corner, Cley, *c. 1890*. At this time Laurence Randall was landlord and there were four licensed victuallers in the village. Two of them advertised their additional occupations to that of mine host. John Anderson of the King's Head was also a lighterman while Henry Pahley of the Fishmonger's Arms ran a commercial and posting house as well as being a 'bird and animal preserver'. (*Author's collection*)

Cley street, *c.* 1950. Much of this road retains its historic integrity and charm, especially its narrowness; because of this it is regarded as a somewhat precarious section of the main coast road in high season. (*Author's collection*)

Cley High Street, *c.* 1955. Nearest to us on the right is the village post and telegraph office in Whalebone House, the flint facings of which are augmented by decorations made from sheep vertebrae. Just beyond, the sign proclaims the Fishmonger's Arms pub described by Walter Rye in 1887 as 'Fair accommodation to the wayfarer and winter wild duck shooter . . . a roomy old-fashioned house.' (*Author's collection*)

Cley marshes, 2001. Today where the wildfowl shooter once stalked his prey ornithologists flock armed with nothing more offensive than high-powered binoculars and telescopes to observe and appreciate this remarkable marshland habitat. The oldest and best known Norfolk Wildlife Trust nature reserve, it was purchased by the trust's founder Dr Sydney Long in 1926. Cley was the first County Nature Reserve in the country and started a national movement of forty-seven wildlife trusts and over 2,000 nature reserves. (*Author's collection*)

The Dun Cow at Salthouse, *c.* 1903. This was a key meeting place for the village. The proprietors of the Broads and Marshes, as well as the Salthouse Stock and Cattle Association, met here. The sturdy flint wall enclosure around the pub garden was not constructed without a purpose: when the tides threatened the marshes the cattle were all removed to the safety of these walls. (*Author's collection*)

3

Holt & District

Spout Hills, Holt, *c.* 1910. Situated on the south-west side of the town, the spring afforded an ample supply of pure soft water which was carried in carts to Holt until the rural sanitary authority erected a brick pumping house in 1885. (*Author's collection*)

The rural idyll of Glandford Mill, 1953. This mill was a typically sturdy construction by Sir Alfred Jodrell and w
built on the site of the old wooden mill which burnt down in 1913. Operating for a number of years under t
Cracknell family, Holbrook & Revell and William West poultry and pig food specialist, it became redundant aft
the Second World War. After falling into decay it was restored and converted into a home for Robin Combe aft
he inherited the Bayfield Hall Estate in 1969/70. (*Norfolk Local Studies Library*)

Glandford shell museum, *c.* 1938. The museum was built on the instructions of Sir Alfred Jodrell by workmen from his estate at nearby Bayfield Hall in 1915. It houses his collection of shells, many of them carved with intricate designs, and other curios collected by Sir Alfred over sixty years. It may be viewed for a small charge, the proceeds being given for many years to the Norfolk and Norwich Hospital. (*Author's collection*)

The Holt road seen from Letheringsett Bridge, *c.* 1905. The picturesque village of Letheringsett is situated in the well-wooded valley of the River Glaven. The bridge seen here was built by subscription in 1818 but much of the shape of the village is the result of the thoughtful planning of William Hardy and his descendants, the notable Norfolk family of Cozens-Hardy, who 'clothed the barren hills with foliage' from the early nineteenth century. (*Author's collection*)

Letheringsett Mill, pictured in 1975, was built in 1802. Mills have stood on the site since the eleventh century. In the foreground is Arthur Rayner who served fifty years in the milling trade – three years at Glandford, the rest at Letheringsett. He was taken on as an apprentice seven months after his fourteenth birthday. In those days both Glandford and Letheringsett mills were owned by the Cracknell family and fourteen men worked in the two mills. When this photograph was taken Mr Rayner was the last man left. The mill was mostly used as a warehouse for feedstuffs with small grinding jobs carried out for local farmers. In 1982 it was restored to full working order and is open to the public. (*Norfolk Local Studies Library*)

Holt High Street, *c.* 1960. The unmistakable round sign of the King's Head pub hangs on the right and just down from there is Betty's outfitters, still familiar to shoppers today. Holt has always been a town to offer a fine diversity of shops. At 20 High Street was Edwards & Kidd which offered childrenswear, dressmaking supplies and handknitted garments as well as bed and breakfast accommodation. (*Eastern Counties Newspapers*)

olt market place, 1960. On the left is the noted Larners Store, truly a Holt institution. Among the other well-membered stores are Knowles the tailor and school outfitter who sold uniforms to Greshams schoolboys for over 00 years and Newmans the newsagent, stockists of Meccano, Dinky toys and Airfix model kits. (*Eastern Counties* *ewspapers*)

hite Lion corner, Holt, *c.* 1965.
vo of the lost pubs of Holt are
en here: the Bullards' White
on Hotel on the right and
eward & Patteson's Star on the
t. Today Holt has a national
putation for quality shops
aling in the best of fabrics,
othes, pottery, furniture, food
d wines. One of the first
portant stores of this type in
e town was situated on White
on Corner. Begun in the 1930s
was called The Blue Room and
as run by Miss Joan Chase. It
owcased and sold a wide variety
goods described as 'up market'
oducts. (*Eastern Counties*
wspapers*)

A morning physical training session at the Norfolk Education Committee's summer camp, Holt Hall, August 1953. Since shortly after the Second World War Holt Hall has been a county educational establishment run initially under the auspices of the Norfolk Education Committee. In the early years it was a kind of private secondary modern school but the NEC also ran camps and fieldwork activities in the grounds. Today it is Norfolk's premier residential field study centre where diverse courses provide education and fun for children and adults throughout the year. (*Author's collection*)

Kelling Sanatorium, *c.* 1910. Opened in 1903, it was intended as a sanatorium 'for consumptive persons unable to pay the high fees charged by private institutions'. Treatment was based on patients' intake of 'fresh air'. The cubicles in the grounds were left with their doors open in even the coldest weather. Patients were expected to do a certain amount of work which could range from one hour cleaning brasses to six hours in the gravel pit. Those not working would take afternoon 'constitutionals' along the Cromer Road – women in the morning, men in the afternoon. (*Author's collection*)

Interior of the Children's Sanatorium, Kelling, *c.* 1913. The Children's Sanatorium was opened as a result of public appeals and voluntary efforts in August 1906 at Bramblewood, a site adjoining the adult sanatorium. The first purpose-built building followed in 1911/12, run under the watchful eye of the matron, Miss Marion Rumball. A contemporary record declared: 'Children come in thin and go away fat, come in miserable and go away gloriously happy and healthy.' Although great efforts were made by the staff to cheer their young wards, many children were left haunted by traumatic experiences and vivid memories for the rest of their lives. (*Muckleburgh Collection*)

Weybourne water mill, *c.* 1912. Pictured here are, left to right: Ellis Beales, the miller, his wife Sarah, Miriam Digby, the housemaid, and Daisy, the daughter of the house. The present mill was built on the seaward side of the village in the early nineteenth century and is shown on Bryant's map of 1826. It and the old post mill were kept in the mid-nineteenth century by John Dawson. This is one of the few mills in the county with an overshot wheel. (*Muckleburgh Collection*)

James Henry Martin (standing), landlord of the Ship Inn, with his wife, seated in their carriage, in front of their pub on what is now the main coast road through Weybourne, *c.* 1910. (*Author's collection*)

Eyes right! Major J.R. Davis, Camp Staff Officer at Weybourne Anti-Aircraft Practice Camp, takes the salute as artillerymen from 12th Battery, Blackdown, Aldershot, march back to camp up Weybourne Street after Sunday church parade on 7 June 1936. The Revd E.C.S. Upcher led the service and was also the camp chaplain. (*Muckleburgh Collection*)

Weybourne Camp, *c.* 1935. Since the earliest threats of aggression by foreign powers Weybourne and its nearby natural harbours have been invasion targets. A famous couplet states: 'He who old England would hope to win, Must at Weybourne hope begin.' As a result, over the years a military presence has been a regular feature of Weybourne life. It came as no surprise to the locals when an anti-aircraft artillery practice camp was established in the clifftops in 1935. (*Author's collection*)

Senior NCOs, Royal Artillery Anti-Aircraft Camp, Weybourne, 1941. During the early war years, notably through one of the coldest winters on record, Weybourne Camp was used by both the Royal Artillery and Territorial soldiers from the 5th Battalion, The Royal Norfolk Regiment, on coastal defence duty. As the war progressed the camp was turned over to anti-aircraft duties and was manned by artillerymen and ladies of the Auxiliary Territorial Service. (*Author's collection*)

Crashed Junkers 88 on Weybourne Beach, 3 May 1941. Hit by anti-aircraft fire near the Wash, this aircraft was forced down 300 yards from Sparrow Gap. The crew escaped with minor injuries and paddled to the shore in their emergency dinghy. They were later arrested and escorted to the Sheringham Hotel before being handed over to the War Department authorities. (*Peter Brooks*)

The Muckleburgh Collection, Weybourne Camp, 1994. After the last gun was fired in 1958 and the camp finally closed in 1959 the site faced an uncertain future. Ideas for a nuclear power plant and a holiday camp were mooted. The site was acquired by Mr C. Berry Savory in the mid-1980s and was formally opened as the Muckleburgh Collection by the Duke of Argyll on 7 May 1988. Today it is the country's largest privately owned working military museum. (*Muckleburgh Collection*)

Weybourne coastguard station, *c.* 1916. The coastguard moved here from its original base on the beach in about 1913. The station was manned by a chief officer and four men and was provided with signal flags, telegraph system and a Board of Trade life-saving rocket apparatus. (*Author's collection*)

Sea Cadets 'On War Service' at Weybourne coastguard station, 1915. (*Muckleburgh Collection*)

Weybourne tower windmill, 2001. It was built in about 1850 and the first miller was Daniel Brett (1850–8). After having a number of owners it finished its working life in the hands of the Youngman family during the First World War. It fell into disrepair but was then partially renovated, mostly to make it habitable as a private residence in the 1920s. It was restored to most of its former glory in the late 1960s and early 1970s, the new cap being made by William Bird & Son of North Walsham in 1968. (*Author's collection*)

4

Sheringham & District

A fine group of 'Shannock' fishermen, *c.* 1902. Left to right they are Potter Hardingham, John 'Tar' Bishop, Elijah Farrow and 'Belcher' Johnson. 'Shannock' is a term which is derived from the old Norfolk word 'Shanny', meaning one who is mad and daring. The term has been adopted and is a name borne with great pride by those whose families have been present in Sheringham for generations and may rightly call themselves 'Shannocks'. (*Author's collection*)

All Saints' Church, Upper Sheringham, *c.* 1905. At this time the village was supplied with fresh water piped from a nearby spring to the reservoir seen on the left. This was built by Abbot Upcher to celebrate the end of the Napoleonic Wars in 1814. Sadly, Bonaparte escaped from Elba and his final defeat was in fact to be a year later at Waterloo. (*Norfolk Local Studies Library*)

Upper Sheringham from Sheringham Road, *c.* 1955. The inhabitants of this little village held the British record for longevity for many years. The eminent London pathologist Dr David Davies believed the reason for this was the rich mixture of trace elements such as iron, calcium, chromium and selenium in the soil from which so much of the local produce came. (*Author's collection*)

retty Corner, Sheringham, *c.* 1930. A 1930s guidebook waxed lyrical about this view: 'A view which has graced
any an artists' canvas and sketchbook. . . . Nestling in its hollow in the distance is Upper Sheringham with its
he church surrounded by ancient cottages, truly an unspoilt hamlet. Here ravine and copse, heather and fern,
llage and church, homestead and rippling field, cliff and skiff are set out in perfect perspective.' To preserve this
ea from building development or industry the council purchased Pretty Corner and its surrounding woodlands
1927. (*Author's collection*)

Beach and fishermen's slipway, Sheringham, *c*. 1955. The first promenades and sea defence works were built here in the late nineteenth century as the popularity of the town grew; by 1896 over £30,000 had been expended. By 1900 the sea wall and promenade extended two-thirds of a mile and in 1909 this was increased by another 113 yards on the eastern side. Following the 1912 floods a raised promenade and shelter were constructed. (*Author's collection*)

The Sheringham lifeboat *Henry Ramey Upcher* with her crew in front of the boat shed on the fishermen's slipway, *c*. 1916. Paid for by the benevolent Upcher family of Sheringham Hall, the vessel was built by well-respected local boat-builder Lewis 'Buffalo' Emery and was launched on 4 September 1894. The *Henry Ramey Upcher* served Sheringham for over forty years and her crews were directly responsible for saving well over 200 lives in the course of sixty-one active launches. This grand old boat has been fully restored and is on display in her old boat shed, which is now a museum. (*Norfolk Local Studies Library*)

Launching the *Henry Ramey Upcher* for spectators, *c.* 1935. When the boat was needed on service two maroons were fired to alert the crew who would race to the shed, fling open the doors and quickly lay the boards on which the boat slid down the slipway, controlled by ropes. When the boat reached the bottom of the slipway, if there was insufficient water to float her she would be moved to the sea on skeets (rollers). Once there the crew scrambled aboard while fishermen pushed her afloat. When she was clear of the beach the mast was stepped and the sail set. (*Author's collection*)

Sheringham lifeboat crewmen on the beach after the launch, *c.* 1935. Left to right: Henry 'Joyful' West, John Cooper, Harry 'Bob' West, Jimmy Bishop, Robert 'Willie' West and John 'Rook' Reynolds. (*Norfolk Local Studies Library*)

Two hardy Sheringham Shannock fishermen, Jimmy Scotter and Jimmy Dunbrel with their crab boat and pots, *c.* 1935. (*Norfolk Local Studies Library*)

Sheringham fishermen brothers 'Billy Cutty' Craske and Teddy Craske bring ashore a basketful of their catch of longshore herring, *c.* 1950. During the late 1940s and early '50s about fifty fishermen worked out of Sheringham on about twenty small motor boats, travelling as far as 8 miles from land and fishing at depths from 3 to 10 fathoms. (*Author's collection*)

'Too-fee' Farrow and Reg Emery in the doorway of Emery's boat-building shed on Lifeboat Plain, *c.* 1948. The Emery family built boats in Sheringham for well over 100 years. Their boats were built 'by eye' with a complete absence of instruments and drawings. They constructed their last boat in 1957. (*Author's collection*)

Leaving Sheringham beach with a television set bought by public subscription for the *Dudgeon* lightship, 1958. Left to right: 'Downtide' West, Eddie Hagues, Cyril Hunt, Bernard Graham, -?-, Billy Cutty jnr, and Mrs F.L. Mason. In the boat are William 'Chris' Craske and T. Craske. (*Norfolk Local Studies Library*)

The Boulevard, Sheringham, *c.* 1912. As the popularity of Sheringham grew, the sleepy fishing village of the nineteenth century became a 'modern' holiday resort of the twentieth century, complete with railway link, commodious hotels, esplanade, promenade and grand boulevard. This is exactly as the great English composer Ralph Vaughan Williams would have known it when he stayed here in 1919. (*Norfolk Local Studies Library*)

Church Street, Sheringham, *c.* 1910. As the fishing hamlet of Lower Sheringham grew it was felt that the resort should have its own church. St Peter's was built between 1895 and 1897 on a site given to the town by the Upcher family. Constructed by Bardell Bros of King's Lynn at a cost of £8,000, it was opened on St Peter's day 1897. (*Author's collection*)

GRAND HOTEL
:: SHERINGHAM ::

Unique Position on Sea Front

Adjoining Golf Links with Private Entrance thereto
All Modern Improvements

Magnificent Ballroom   -   Electric Lift

Large Sheltered Gardens with Sun Gallery, Tennis Courts, Putting Green, etc. OWN GARAGE with Lock-up Boxes.

The Public Rooms are the largest and most comfortable on the East Coast with Spacious Lounges Overlooking the Sea.

Safe Sea Bathing from Hotel or Hotel Beach Tents.
NOTED FOR CUISINE AND SERVICE.

Terms Reasonable especially in May, June and July

For Tariff apply: **P. T. GREEN, Manager.**

Tel. Sheringham 1   Telegrams: Grand Hotel,
  (2 Lines)   Sheringham.

The Grand and Burlington Hotels are under the same Management and are the only Hotels on the Sea Front

Under the same direction: ORCHARD HOTEL, PORTMAN ST. W.1. and NEWLANDS HOTEL, RUSSELL SQUARE, W.C. 1.

Advertisement for the Grand Hotel, Sheringham, *c.* 1937. Along with the Burlington and Sheringham hotels it was one of the premier establishments built in the town for society visitors in the 1890s. As the great age of coastal holidays faded in the wake of two world wars the Grand was converted to holiday flats. Falling into a tragic decline, it was finally demolished in 1974. (*Author's collection*)

Church Street, Sheringham, c. 1910. As the village grew into a town and resort, given responsibility as a self-governing urban district in 1901, its popularity and wealth were displayed in the fine façades of the new shops. Here is a fine example – the painted glass and gilded lettering on the front of James Ardley's grocers, photographed complete with his delivery car. (*Norfolk Local Studies Library*)

Sheringham High Street, 1961. Most of the Victorian and Edwardian shop façades remain above street level but several of the shopfronts with their long panelled windows and pull-down blinds have been modernised in typical 1950s and '60s style to have wide glass windows with aluminium surrounds and plastic signs. Businesses seen here include Green & Wright wine and spirit merchants, Jordan's chemist, George Youngs (Farms) Ltd butchers and Craske's restaurant. (*Eastern Counties Newspapers*)

Sheringham High Street seen from the bottom of Station Road, *c.* 1955. On the left is the fondly remembered Rusts Ltd, drapers and milliners. On the right is the old town reservoir built in 1862, complete with the town clock. The structure is known locally as the 'Mary Pym' after the lady who presented the clock to the town as an Easter gift in 1903. Still in evidence in 1955 is the old town trough for watering horses; there was once a lower, smaller trough on the left-hand side for dogs. Restored in 1989 by a team of volunteers and fitted with windows and seats, today it provides a restful stopping point for visitors and locals. (*Author's collection*)

Murder and mayhem on the cards for a summer season at Sheringham's Little Theatre in the 1970s. This gem of a playhouse was opened after the closure of the old town cinema in 1959. With support and funding from North Norfolk District Council the theatre continues to entertain, with live shows in the summer from touring companies and local amateur groups, and films in the winter. Its future looks good after its 1997 refurbishment made possible by £280,000 of National Lottery funding. (*Sheringham Little Theatre*)

The Mayflower, a magnificent float at the Sheringham carnival, 'sails' up the high street in 1976. Sheringham's carnival week dates back to 1948. The regatta and sports revived the previous year were so popular it was decided to hold a carnival week of activities, dances and a grand parade of decorated floats. (*Norfolk Local Studies Library*)

A 'members' train' approaches Weybourne station in the early days of the North Norfolk Railway, *c.* 1974. The preservation society was formed as the result of a scheme to save the Midland & Great Northern Railway in 1959. By 1966 the preservationists had raised just enough money to save the section of track between Sheringham and Weybourne. The railway operated members' only trains until it was granted permission to run under BR supervision in 1975. In 1976 it was granted its own light railway order by Parliament and has grown to become one of the largest tourist attractions in the county, carrying more than 100,000 passengers a year. In 1989 the rebuilt line from Weybourne to Holt was reopened. (*North Norfolk Railway*)

Beeston Regis Priory and abbey farmhouse, 1971. Founded by Lady Isabel de Cressey in 1216, this was an Augustinian Priory dedicated to St Mary the Virgin. It was endowed with a manor, certain land, services and a fishery. Its income was never great but it maintained a dignified religious simplicity. Falling, along with most other religious houses, at the Dissolution in the mid-sixteenth century, today its remains consist of a 130ft church and remnants of cloisters. (*Author's collection*)

Sir Thomas Cook, the affectionately remembered County Commissioner of Norfolk St John Ambulance, talks to cadets on parade at county summer camp, Beeston Regis, August 1962. To his right is another well-remembered and respected county officer of the time, Anne Ettridge, whose name was synonymous with St John county camps. (*Norfolk St John Ambulance Archive*)

West Runton Common, *c.* 1908. On the left is the Runton Links Hotel, built in 1890. It was named after its renowned golf links designed by J.H. Taylor, Open Champion golfer 1894, 1895 and 1900. A total of 6,125 yards in length, it was hailed as 'one of the most sporting golf courses in Great Britain'. Green fees in 1947 were: July and September 4s a day, 21s a week; August 5s a day, 25s a week; and for the rest of the year 3s per day and 17s 6d a week. (*Author's collection*)

The restored Early English-style church of Holy Trinity and its fine lychgate (built in 1886), West Runton, *c.* 1910. (*Author's collection*)

The Village Inn, West Runton, *c.* 1955. This hostelry, popular with locals, holidaymakers and visitors passing through on the main coast road between Sheringham and Cromer, was opened in 1927. It still had a well-maintained putting green when this picture was taken; time has moved on and the lovingly kept green is now dotted with picnic tables for *al fresco* drinking and dining – and very pleasant it is too! (*Author's collection*)

The Street, West Runton, *c.* 1950. Although not as big as Cromer or Sheringham, West Runton is a seaside village with a strong orientation towards the holiday trade. When the railway link came it was even suggested that the village 'bids fair to prove a serious rival to its larger neighbours on either hand'. But in a very similar way to Mundesley this simply did not happen. (*Author's collection*)

The Gap and tea rooms, West Runton, *c.* 1935. The holiday camps near here are viewed with mixed feelings by villagers, especially since a successful challenge to the old tradition by which the caravans were removed in the winter months. This was founded on the belief that these were 'half-year' lands which had to be free for grazing animals between October and April each year. (*Norfolk Local Studies Library*)

Roman Camp Tea Gardens, West Runton, *c.* 1935. The Roman Camp is an area of outstanding natural beauty. A 1930s guide described it in glowing terms: 'Nowhere is it possible to find a spot richer in the colour of its trees, bracken and furze.' This area was given to the National Trust in September 1924. The name Roman Camp is something of a misnomer; there is no evidence of Roman occupation here and the title only goes back to the turn of the twentieth century. The archaeological remains here are in fact iron workings from the Saxon and early medieval periods. (*Norfolk Local Studies Library*)

A technical hitch meant Mr M.J. Sainty had to climb up to assist Ian Wallace when the West Runton village sign was unveiled in September 1977. (*Norfolk Local Studies Library*)

East Runton High Street, *c.* 1950. This is one half of the two wards in the ecclesiastical parish of Runton (the other being West Runton). The changes to the village between 1900 and 1950 rendered it almost unidentifiable to anyone who knew the fishing hamlet here before the turn of the century. It acted as an overflow for Cromer and Sheringham, and many of the terraced houses and shops here were built specifically for the holiday trade. Within the forty years between 1890 and 1930 the combined population of East and West Runton rose from 506 to 1,080. (*Norfolk Local Studies Library*)

East Runton caravan site café, *c.* 1950. In the latter years of the nineteenth and early years of the twentieth century thousands had their imaginations captured by stories of 'Poppyland'. Train brochures and holiday guides took great pains to entreat people to 'Come to Poppyland'. It was along these cliffs towards Cromer and beyond into Sidestrand that people would walk by their thousand through the summer months, breathing the sea air and admiring the swaying crimson fields of poppies. Alas the poppies were allowed to disappear almost unnoticed, for in the 1920s and '30s white tents began to spring up over the hills and eventually caravan parks replaced the fields where the flowers once danced. (*Norfolk Local Studies Library*)

Cromer Road, East Runton, *c.* 1955. (*Norfolk Local Studies Library*)

5

Cromer

Fisherman 'Tuna' Harrison admires a fine bunch of Cromer crabs, April 1975. (*Norfolk Local Studies Library*)

West Cliff, Cromer, *c.* 1906. In the ten years before his death in 1892 Benjamin Bond Cabbell did much to promote the development of the growing seaside town by selling portions of the Cromer Hall estate adjoining Norwich Road and on the west side of the town along the Runton Road behind the West Cliff. This made land available for the construction of fine holiday apartment buildings and most notably the great hotels 'With extensive sea views' for visiting gentry along Runton Road. (*Author's collection*)

Runton Road, *c.* 1949. The great hotels built by speculators in the 1890s were given names like The Grand (1891) and The Cliftonville (1894), and were designed by premier architects such as George Skipper of Norwich. These establishments never recovered their popularity after the Second World War. The depression of the postwar years followed by the advent of package holidays sealed their fate – demolition or conversion to flats and 'modern' hotels. The West Cliff area itself underwent conversion to pleasure gardens in the early twentieth century and is today decorated with gay flowerbeds and strings of multi-coloured lights and illuminated seaside images. (*Author's collection*)

East Cliff, Cromer, 1887. Much of the land in the foreground has been lost to coastal erosion. Jutting out to sea is the old timber jetty built in 1846. Bathing machines, sailing craft and simple beach entertainment indicate an unspoilt resort loved by the gentlefolk enticed here by the writings of Clement Scott, the creator of 'Poppyland', in those halcyon days before the First World War. (*Author's collection*)

The view enjoyed by promenaders from the jetty, *c.* 1895. The magnificent building spread along the sea front is the Hotel de Paris, pictured shortly after its facelift in 1894, courtesy of the designs of George Skipper. The hotel was originally Lord Suffield's grand summer residence. It became a hotel in 1830 when Pierre le François took it over. Probably the most famous of all the Cromer hotels, in its heyday at the beginning of the twentieth century it hosted numerous notable visitors including members of the German royal family. (*Author's collection*)

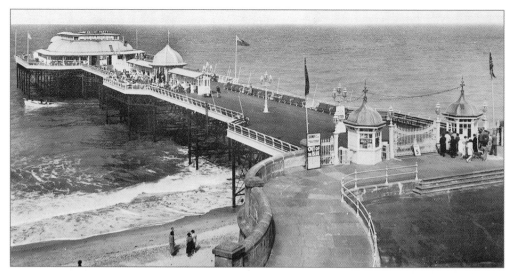

Cromer Pier, *c.* 1935. In 1897 the old jetty was wrecked by a storm and dismantled. On 8 June 1901 the new pier was opened by Lord Claude Hamilton, Chairman of the Great Eastern Railway Company. It was originally headed by a bandstand, but the Pavilion Theatre was developed between 1905 and 1912. The gates at the entrance to the pier were taken for scrap during the war and the delightful kiosks either side were replaced with a new structure with a unified high-pitched tiled roof. After enduring a number of years with a flat roof, placed there after damage incurred in the 1953 floods, the entrance was restyled and the domes replaced in 1989. (*Author's collection*)

A free afternoon on the pier, June 1955. Left to right: Mr J. Webster, Chairman of the Pier Committee, Mr W.H. Gaston and Mr T. Makins of the Pier Committee and 'Matty' Nockells who at the time had served thirty-three years as Cromer's Beach and Traffic Inspector. When it opened in 1901, entrance to the pier cost 1*d*, rising to 2*d* by 1904. Entrance to the bandstand enclosure was 2*d* extra. By 1964 charges were 4*d* for adults and 2*d* for children. Admission charges were finally abolished in 1984. (*Author's collection*)

Since 1978 Cromer Pier Pavilion Theatre has run a 'Summer Special' as its main holiday period feature. Seen here is the company of 'Seaside Special '80'. Left to right: Ann Emery, Lee Reynolds, Barry Daniels, Ros Murray, Frankie Holmes, Julia Burnett, Gordon Glenn, Linda Hering, Betty Ann Ransford, David Ransford and Hilary Wedgwood. (*Norfolk Local Studies Library*)

On the night of Sunday 14 November 1993 a jack-up platform called 'Tayjack 1', which was being used up the coast in the construction of Anglian Water's long sea outfall, had its legs shorn off by stormy seas. Carried towards Cromer, it smashed through the pier. Work began almost immediately to restore the old pier. Just fourteen weeks later reconstruction and restoration was complete and the pier was reopened by Gillian Shepherd MP on 1 May 1994. (*Eastern Counties Newspapers*)

Cromer crab fishermen landing their boats on the East Beach at the bottom of the gangway, 1951. Fishermen returning with their catch run their boats straight for the beach; the helmsman gives the boat a sheer just before she strikes and the crew fling themselves to the inshore side of the boat, thus throwing her over so that the waves bash harmlessly (it is hoped) against her bottom. Meanwhile men ashore hook the boat up to a tractor and drag it out of harm's way so that the catch can be landed. (*Author's collection*)

Fishing boats, crab and lobster pots at the bottom of the East Gangway, Cromer, 1951. Fishermen usually made their own crab pots. Traditionally the pots had an iron-framed base with a heavy iron bottom which was called a 'music' because it resembled a piano keyboard. The hoops and bars were made of hazel cut from local hedgerows and the net was braided from manila hemp or 'pot stuff'. (*Author's collection*)

Fishermen mending their nets and pots in Cromer, 1954. Five-year-old Billy Davies (left) and six-year-old Tony Harrison watch Dick Davies and George Lusher repairing a pot and a marker buoy. (*Author's collection*)

Norman Everitt, Bob Davies and his wife Gladys preparing the morning catch of Cromer crabs for market, May 1959. The name of Davies seems to have been associated with Cromer fishing since time immemorial. Bob Davies opened his crab stall before the war and ran it for well over fifty years, a tradition his family proudly carries on today. (*Author's collection*)

Hundreds gather to watch the launch of Cromer lifeboat, *c.* 1908. The boat was the *Louisa Heartwell*. Powered by oarsmen and sail, this was the vessel that was to figure in the earliest exploits of Henry Blogg. (*Author's collection*)

Rescue of the crew of the *Sepoy*, 13 December 1933. The 65-ton barge was driven ashore 200 yards off Cromer. The Cromer No. 1 boat was on another service and Cromer people watched with horror as the *Sepoy* sank and the two-man crew climbed the rigging and lashed themselves to the mast. The reserve lifeboat *Alexandra* was launched with a crew whose average age was sixty. After attempts to attach lines failed Coxswain Henry Blogg took the daring decision to drive his lifeboat over the sunken decks to rescue the crew, an act he had to carry out twice – snatching one crew member each pass! With the rescue complete but the lifeboat short of fuel there was no alternative but to drive for safety by beaching the boat on the Cromer shoreline. (*Norfolk Local Studies Library*)

Henry Blogg GC (1876–1954), Coxswain of the Cromer lifeboat for thirty-eight years with fifty-three years service in all. He joined the Cromer lifeboat in 1894 when he was eighteen and was made coxswain at the age of thirty-three. During his years of service the Cromer lifeboat went out 387 times saving 873 lives. His actions in rescuing men from stricken vessels such as *Fernebo*, *Sepoy*, *Porthcawl* and *English Trader* became legendary. Awarded the RNLI gold medal (the lifeboatman's VC) three times and three silver medals, he was also presented with the George Cross and the British Empire Medal. The greatest of all the lifeboatmen, he was quite simply one of the bravest men who ever lived. Like a lot of Norfolk heroes Henry Blogg hated fuss and really didn't like to recount tales of heroism to public audiences; he preferred to keep his medals in a box in the kitchen dresser rather than be seen wearing them. (*Author's collection*)

Old crewmates await the arrival of the cortège at the funeral of Henry Blogg GC, Cromer, Thursday 17 June 1954. About 1,400 people crammed into the parish church and outside another 1,000 waited in the churchyard forming a square at least five deep around the church wall. The coast had never seen a funeral quite like it, nor a man held in such universal high regard. (*Norfolk Local Studies Library*)

Unveiling the plaque in the Henry Blogg Memorial shelter, August 1955. Left to right: Lord Templewood, Mr Graveling, Chairman of the Urban District Council, and Mr J. Smith and Mr M.J.N. van der Hiddle who were rescued by Henry Blogg early in his service with the RNLI. (*Author's collection*)

Probably the honour that would have pleased Henry Blogg most was to have the new Cromer lifeboat named after him. It is seen here with Blogg's nephew Coxswain Henry 'Shrimp' Davies at the helm after going to the aid of the *Francois Tixier* on 8 July 1948. (*Eastern Counties Newspapers*)

The Cromer No. 2 lifeboat being towed in by tractor after a test launch following its overhaul and the refitting of a radio, *c.* 1950. (*Author's collection*)

Tuesday 13 August 1963 and the country was gripped by the story of the Great Train Robbery, but a fi distraction was provided by the lifeboat and air sea rescue display to mark Lifeboat Day in Cromer. Mast Signaller Leach is on the line from the helicopter; having retrieved the dummy from the water, he is delivering it Cromer No. 1 lifeboat. (*Eastern Counties Newspapers*)

Coxswain Richard Davis (far left) and his crew of Cromer lifeboatmen after almost eigh hours at sea attending the collision between the Hamburg-based EMS *Ferry* and the Belgian coaster *Und* off Great Yarmouth on 30 January 1981. (*Eastern Counties Newspapers*)

West Beach and Melbourne Slope, *c.* 1935. On the beach and up the slope are the boats of the West Beach fishermen with their crab pots. Tows (ropes and floats) are just visible on the rails towards the bottom of the slope. The slopes and esplanade were begun on the East Beach area in 1894 primarily as sea defences. Under a further scheme of sea defences and to improve beach access, in 1900/01 the Western and Eastern Esplanades were connected to form one promenade. Along with the sea wall this complete scheme cost the huge sum of £34,000. (*Author's collection*)

Cromer High Street, *c.* 1950. On the left is the High Street entrance of the Hotel de Paris and on the right is the King's Head when it was still a Steward & Patteson pub. Towering above it all, and visible for miles around, is the 160ft tower of St Peter and St Paul's Church. (*Author's collection*)

Thomas Cook's Lobster Coach trotting along Church Street, *c.* 1910. So called because it carried lobsters from Cromer to Norwich, this service was described as a 'gentleman's whimsey', harking back to the 'Golden Age of Coaching'. It ran from August 1909 until shortly before the First World War. The fare was 10*s* single or 12*s* 6*d* return. The trip set out from the Grand Hotel, Cromer, and changed horses at Roughton, Aylsham and St Faiths on its way to the Maid's Head Hotel, Norwich. On its return the coach stopped for tea at the Black Boys Inn, Aylsham. The complete trip took about 2½ hours. (*Author's collection*)

William Churchyard & Sons' West End Supply Stores, Prince of Wales Road, *c.* 1904. Mr Churchyard built this business on the site of an old house which was home to Dr Earle and Dr Flunder in the early nineteenth century. West End Supply Stores was sold to the Co-op shortly before the First World War. (*Norfolk Local Studies Library*)

Church Street, *c.* 1905. On the left is East House which was established as a hairdressers and tobacconists in 1820. It was owned by Tommy Clarke in the 1930s but when a stick of bombs was dropped on Church Street in 1942 one scored a direct hit, killing Tommy's sister. This is now the site of the Henry Blogg memorial garden and shelter. (*Author's collection*)

The junction of Chapel Street, Church Street and Garden Street, *c.* 1948. On the left is the Workers Canteen which has now been demolished to enable the road to be widened. On the right is the shop of Harry H. Tansley who also had another store on Augusta Street, Sheringham. He was without doubt the finest and most prolific social documentary photographer of the North Norfolk coast. (*Author's collection*)

West Beach, 1962. Many gents with suits and ties simply take off their jackets and roll up their shirtsleeves to effect instant beach wear. Ladie wear A-line skirts with printed flowers or checks and complete their look with a cardigan thrown across the shoulders – how things have changed (*Norfolk Local Studies Library*)

Crowds filled with smiles watch the final leg of the waiters' race, a traditional feature of the Cromer carnival celebrations, as competitors approach the pier, September 1962. (*Norfolk Local Studies Library*)

Cave men, women, boys and girls by their float after the parade at Cromer carnival, August 1977. Many readers will probably remember the well-crafted triceratops on display in front of the little dinosaur and fossil museum on Prince of Wales Road. (*Norfolk Local Studies Library*)

Some very hairy ladies strike a pose for the camera after the bed race at the carnival, 1977. Carnivals and fetes have been regular features of Cromer life since the 1920s. Growing into a week of dances, fetes, parades, races and special events it is probably the biggest carnival celebration in Norfolk, and is visited by people from all over the county and beyond. (*Norfolk Local Studies Library*)

Cromer Hall, *c.* 1910. The original hall on this site burnt down in 1829 before it could be completed. Rebuilt by Mr G. Windham, the hall was sold in 1852 to Benjamin Bond Cabbell in whose family it remains to this day. At the turn of the century Mrs Bond-Cabbell, lady of the manor of Cromer, allowed visitors to explore her grounds by presenting a ticket obtained from Messrs Jarrold or the Library of Mr Dulley of Church Street. A charge of sixpence was made for the benefit of the Cromer District Nurse Fund. (*Author's collection*)

Cromer Lighthouse, situated 250ft up on the East Cliffs, *c.* 1905. The first lighthouse was built in 1719, replacing a beacon which used to be lit on top of the church tower. It was lost in 1866 when the land on which it stood succumbed to coastal erosion. In anticipation of this event, Trinity House had this replacement built in 1832. It has an electric light of 49,000 candle power and on a clear day it can be seen from almost 23 miles out to sea. (*Author's collection*)

6

'Poppyland' to Bacton

Eastern Belle passing through Gunton on her return journey from Cromer, 1930. From the turn of the century London to Cromer could be achieved on summertime express trains in 175 minutes. (*Author's collection*)

Children inspect a section of cliff at Cromer Golf Course which had begun to slide and was liable to fall into the sea at any moment, May 1962. The battle against coastal erosion is constantly being fought with groyne systems, sea walls and defences installed along the North Norfolk coast. In the section of coastline between Cromer and Overstrand alone the fishing communities and towns of Shipden, Clare, Foulness and Beckhythe have all succumbed and have been washed away since the twelfth century. (*Norfolk Local Studies Library*)

The two churches of Overstrand, *c.* 1950. On the right is the church of St Martin, originally built in the early years of the fifteenth century. It was reduced in size in the early years of the mid-eighteenth century and was half bricked up. The east end was turfed and used as a burial ground for the Buxton family. In 1859 the poor state of the old church and the growing congregation prompted the decision to construct a new building in the churchyard and duly in 1867 Christ Church (seen here on the left) was dedicated. In 1911 the larger church of St Martin was required for the ever-growing congregation and the old church was rebuilt, enlarged and re-dedicated in May 1914. Poor Christ Church was eventually left to decay and was demolished after the Second World War. (*Author's collection*)

Overstrand Hall, *c.* 1930. Originally a farmhouse, greatly enlarged and converted to designs by Lutyens in 1900, this was the home of Lord and Lady Hillingdon. From 1932 until its recent sale it was used as the Leicester Convalescent Home. (*Author's collection*)

Overstrand High Street, *c.* 1935. In the background are the distinctive gables of Sea Marge, built shortly after the beginning of the twentieth century. It was owned by Sir Edgar Speyer, a German banker who was reputed to be a millionaire. In fact at the turn of the century Overstrand was known as the village of millionaires, with no fewer than six living in a community of a little over 400 people. Sir Edgar is remembered as being generous to the fishermen and old folk, even throwing many a party for local children. He left Overstrand when the First World War broke out in 1914. The Sea Marge became a grand hotel; restored in 1996 to its former glory it serves that purpose again today. (*Author's collection*)

The Pleasaunce, *c.* 1910. The hard-working Liberal MP Cyril Flower, Lord Battersea, and his wife Constance, a daughter of Sir Anthony de Rothschild, decided to live here. On the recommendation of Lord Suffield they purchased two villas (1897–9) which the young Edwin Lutyens converted into the grand residence known as The Pleasaunce. The grounds, designed by Gertrude Jekyll and entitled 'the Garden of Dreams' to complement the nearby 'Garden of Sleep', were opened to the public during afternoons in the holiday season for a fee of 6*d* which was donated to charity. After Lady Battersea's death in 1931 half the beautiful gardens were sold to Chivers Ltd for growing fruit, while the house became Christian Endeavour holiday accommodation. (*Author's collection*)

Overstrand Gymkhana, August 1956. David Holmes on Trixie is first past the post in the open potato race. Potatoes heaped up at the start would be passed to the rider as he or she rode up and down the course. The rider would fill a bucket at the other end of the course with the vegetables. Unfortunately, the ponies often ate the potatoes before they reached the bucket! (*Author's collection*)

Surrounded by fields blanketed by crimson poppies, this was 'The Garden of Sleep', based around the ruins of St Michael's Church, Sidestrand. This was the idyllic heart of 'Poppyland' created and eulogized by Clement Scott in his series of articles 'Poppyland – by a holidaymaker written at a farmhouse by the sea' which appeared in the *Daily Telegraph*. His works, combined with the arrival of the railway, made Cromer one of the most fashionable resorts for gentlefolk of the late Victorian and Edwardian era. In a powerfully ironic coincidence the flower of English manhood was being slaughtered on the Somme in 1916 when 'The Garden of Sleep' tumbled over the cliff edge, smashing on to the sands below and into the sea; nothing was ever quite the same again. (*Author's collection*)

Northrepps Cottage, *c.* 1904. Here lived Anna Gurney, the indomitable cripple, scholar and philanthropist. Together with her cousin Sarah Buxton she founded the Belfry School in Overstrand in 1830, so named after the belfry of the local church where lessons were given before the school was built. She was buried in Overstrand church in 1857 and is in good company there with Sir Thomas Fowell Buxton of Northrepps Hall, who died in 1845 and had fought alongside Sir William Wilberforce for the abolition of the slave trade. (*Author's collection*)

George Cubitt Jnr (holding the measure beside the mangolds and pointing), of Beacon Farm, Trimingham, featured on an advertising card for Hadfield's Fertilizer, *c.* 1905, which took pains to quote him as saying: 'I am very pleased with your Manures, having a fine lot of mangolds, some of them weighing 30lbs each. They were grown on the highest point in Norfolk, which speaks well for your Manures.' (*Author's collection*)

iddle Street, Trimingham, *c.* 1910. Peace, quiet and rural tranquillity: all the fishing hamlets and villages along
e North Norfolk coast were like this once. (*Author's collection*)

In October 1953 Britain's last minefield left over from the Second World War was cleared at Trimingham. The No. 1 Bomb Disposal Unit charged with the task consisted of Captain R.H. Hough, Sergeant Major E. Thomas, Sergeant J. Laverty, ten British civilian workers and seven German ex-prisoners of war. The job was made particularly difficult by the fact that most of the mines were not on the beach but were set into the soft cliff face and, as ever, there was no map to help identify where they were set. The photograph shows Sgt Laverty examining some of the additional stray mines and munitions recovered from the surrounding land. (*Norfolk Local Studies Library*)

Another successful detonation for the No. 1 Bomb Disposal Unit, Trimingham, October 1953. Mined areas had to be meticulously searched with detectors. Once a mine was found it was exposed by means of a bricklayer's trowel; a hole was scraped out beside it and the position clearly marked. At the end of the day explosive charges were placed beside the mines, a three-minute safety fuse lit and the 65lb anti-invasion mine would be destroyed. It was anticipated that thousands of mines would be found along the coastline between Trimingham and Overstrand. The work of the unit continued for three years. (*Norfolk Local Studies Library*)

A designated 'Quiet Lane' near Gimingham, 2001. The 'Quiet Lane' scheme has been in place since June 2000. Only the second of its kind in the country, it aims to make a small network of North Norfolk lanes safer for walkers, cyclists and horse riders by encouraging vehicles to use other routes or travel with greater care. No one on 'Quiet Lanes' has priority and all users must be considerate towards each other. The scheme seems to be working well so far, in its own quiet way. (*Author's collection*)

The new post office, Trunch, *c.* 1905. The post office opened as part of Robert Young's shop; he was the village sub-postmaster for the next twenty years. Letters arrived from the North Walsham sorting office twice daily at 6.30am and 3.30pm but there was only one delivery per day. Those who wished to obtain their 3.30 post had to call at the shop to collect it. (*Author's collection*)

Trunch village, 1962. Set back just a few miles from the busy coast road, away from the demands of tourism and traffic, the sleepy village of Trunch has managed to preserve much of its rural tranquillity. Although things changed in the later twentieth century, for generations family names and trades were synonymous with the village, including Bullen carpenter and well-sinker; Gibbons the wheelwright, thatcher and carpenter; Steward the blacksmith; and the Primrose family who ran the brewery and could trace their family history in the village back to the fifteenth century. Presiding over it all is the noble church of St Botolph. In the late nineteenth century straw was put on the floor of the church to keep it warm. During the same period Daniel Holl, the Church Clerk and Verger, regularly brought his water cart to clean the church before he locked it up at night. (*Author's collection*)

Opposite: Smile! The boys and group leaders of the 2nd and 5th Boy Reserves at the Norwich Companies Boys' Brigade Camp, Mundesley, 1920. (*Author's collection*)

orwich companies of the Boys' Brigade at Mundesley Camp, 1913. Mundesley was always a popular venue for
hristian-based youth organizations to have their camps. Away from the 'temptations, vulgarities, minstrels and
awkers' of more commercial local resorts, Mundesley offered good wholesome country living with plenty of sea air
hich, it was hoped, 'purged the young minds of other less comely distractions indulged by youths'. (*Author's collection*)

A milestone in the development of the North Norfolk coastal holiday industry, Mundesley Holiday Camp wa opened by Victor Edwards in 1933 as the first purpose-built, fully catering holiday camp in the country. (*Norfc Local Studies Library*)

Mundesley Sanatorium, pictured here in about 1950, was opened on 2 February 1899 for the treatment consumptive patients by Norfolk & Norwich Hospital physician Dr Frederick Burton Fanning. It was set in 25 acr of land and sheltered paths of different gradients were arranged in the fir woods. These, the long veranda in fro of the sanatorium and specially constructed shelters in the grounds ensured patients passed their days in the op air. (*Author's collection*)

The church of All Saints, Mundesley, seen here in ruins in 1885. It was described as a 'little church with a pyramid roof'. Under the energetic leadership of the Revd Thomas Tegg Harvey the church was restored in 1903–4. A new organ, choir stall and fittings were provided and paid for by public subscription and donations from local gentry. (*Author's collection*)

A bustling Cromer Road, Mundesley, *c.* 1914. Although the traffic may have changed, the road is just as busy today. Along its length are some of the guest houses which sprung up at the turn of the century as Mundesley enjoyed some of the spin-off custom from 'Poppyland' and earned a reputation of being something of a health resort. The gable end just before the church in the distance is the Coronation Hall, still used for village functions and entertainments today. It was built in 1911 by Sidney Randell, a local builder, for £700, which included the laying out of a bowling green. (*Norfolk Local Studies Library*)

The Royal Hotel   A.A.   R.A.C.
(THE HOME OF NELSON)   **Mundesley-on-Sea**
                                    TELEPHONE 350

Free House   **Fully Licensed**
Worthington - Whitbread - Truman - Younger
Indcoope   -   Watneys Ales - Draught Guinness
Good Service and Foods   -   Good Wines
OPEN ALL THE YEAR

THE IDEAL FAMILY HOTEL
100 YARDS FROM BEACH

Hot and Cold Water in all Bedrooms
Comfortable Lounge; and
THE NELSON ROOM
(The Wonder Bar of East Anglia)

Under the Personal Supervision of **Mr. P. J. Boswell**

Mundesley station pictured shortly after it opened in 1898. The station was designed by Cornish and Gaymer ecclesiastical builders and general contractors of North Walsham. When the line was extended via Trimingham and Overstrand to Cromer in 1906, the North Norfolk railway 'loop' was complete. Never quite enjoying the levels of trade anticipated, Mundesley did not become a seaside resort like Cromer or Sheringham. In 1964 the final trains left Mundesley station and less than a year later the buildings and land were sold for £12,150. Today just about all traces of the station have disappear and there is no impression left that the railway ever can here at all. (*Author's collection*)

Advertisement for the Royal Hotel, Paston Road, Mundesley, 1948. Familiar to generations of visitors, th and the Manor House and the Grand were the established hotels of Mundesley. The Royal Hotel still ha a bar decked out with pictures and nautical memorabili in honour of Admiral Lord Nelson who is said to have stayed at the hostelry when it was known as New Inn while he was a child on holiday from the Paston Schoo North Walsham. (*Author's collection*)

Mundesley post office, *c.* 1953. The building was originally built as an estate office for Thomas Wakeling. After passing through other hands it was sold to become the permanent home of Mundesley post office in 1910. The sub-postmaster was Norton T. Wakeling, son of Thomas who had erected the building some forty years earlier! The old saying of what goes around comes around could not be more apt, for Norton was to be sub-postmaster for the next forty years. (*Author's collection*)

Coastguard watch house, putting green and slopes to the beach, Mundesley, *c.* 1947. This is still a smartly kept area of well-painted shelters and cut lawns. The putting green has gone and the coastguard watch house, erected by the Board of Trade in 1928, is now a tiny museum of local history (opened in 1995) and a station of the National Coastwatch Institution. (*Author's collection*)

Girls on an outing from St Augustine's School, Norwich, have a paddle in one of the pools on Mundesley Beach, 1924. (*Norfolk Local Studies Library*)

Mundesley Water Mill, *c.* 1909. Like Weybourne Mill, Mundesley's was powered by a rare overshot waterwheel. Throughout the nineteenth century and until it closed in 1953 the mill was worked by successive generations of the Larter family. Tragically the mill was so badly damaged by fire it had to be demolished in November 1956. (*Author's collection*)

Stow Mill, Paston, *c.* 1910. Built by James Gaze in 1827, it passed to his son Thomas Stearns Gaze a year later. Thomas worked the mill until his death in 1872. It was then run by his son until 1906 and when the latter died it was purchased by Mrs M.A. Harper and was run by her cousin Thomas Livermore until it ceased to operate in 1930. Sold and gutted to become a private residence it was restored again in the 1970s and '80s and today is open to the public. (*Norfolk Local Studies Library*)

Replacing one of the rotten beams in the roof of Paston Barn, July 1975. The 400-year-old barn, one of the oldest and largest in the county, was built for the Paston family in 1581. When this photograph was taken large areas of thatch had been removed to reveal rotten timbers being supported by thatch rather than the other way around. The main reconstruction works were carried out by T.H. Blyth & Son, specialist contractors of Foulsham, with the thatching carried out by Bob Farman and his team from North Walsham. (*Norfolk Local Studies Library*)

Interior of Paston Barn by the distinguished Norfolk photographer Hallam Ashley, April 1954. Probably built by the same craftsmen who constructed Trunch and Knapton churches, Paston Barn has an alternate tie beam and hammer beam roof. It is 160ft long, 24ft wide and about 60ft from floor to roof apex. (*Norfolk Local Studies Library*)

Fisherman's Gap and Cable Hut, Bacton, *c.* 1910. The village of Bacton is an amalgam of the hamlets of Bacton, Bacton Green, Bromholm and Keswick. Significant encroachments have been made here by the sea, especially during great storms in 1836 and 1845. Keswick is recorded as having a church in 1382; today it has been reduced to only a handful of houses because of coastal erosion. (*Author's collection*)

The Duke of Edinburgh pub, Bacton, *c.* 1905. In front of the pub is the delivery cart, with driver and errand boy, from Cubitt & Son, grocers and drapers of North Walsham. At the turn of the century the pub was kept by Richard Francis Proudfoot, who enlarged it to make a family and commercial hotel which offered horses and traps for hire. Proudfoot's butchery was next door. (*Author's collection*)

The post office, Bacton, *c.* 1912. The sub-postmaster here for many years at the beginning of the twentieth century was George Webster. He ran the business as a post office stores in which he acted as grocer, draper, boot and shoe warehouse, patent medicine vendor, fancy repository and methylated spirit vendor. (*Norfolk Local Studies Library*)

Edenhall, Bacton, 1950. It was built in the closing years of the nineteenth century and in 1900 it was known as Eden Lodge, a building of holiday apartments run by Margaret Harvey. By 1904 it had been developed yet further into apartments and boarding house with its own tennis lawn. After the First World War it was known by its old name of Eden Lodge, and part of it was then used as consulting rooms for George L. Barker, physician and surgeon. By 1937 it had returned to being Eden Hall Private Hotel with Mr S. Brigg as proprietor. During the war it was used as a base for the various military units trained in the area. In the postwar years it enjoyed mixed fortunes, passing through a number of hands. It was demolished in the 1990s. (*Author's collection*)

Scott's caravan estate, Bacton, *c.* 1948. After the Second World War Bacton was still an attractive and quiet fishing hamlet, hardly touched by holidaymakers. Scott's estate was probably the first caravan park in the village. The quiet was disturbed when the Bacton gas site was instigated during the 1960s. Although peaceful today the landscape just beyond the village is horribly marred by a large industrial site with two great pylons towering skyward. (*Norfolk Local Studies Library*)

The gatehouse arch of Bromholm Priory, Bacton, *c.* 1900. This was a Cluniac priory founded in 1113 by William de Glanville. It was said to have a portion of the True Cross which performed miraculous cures and pilgrims came here from all over the country. Bromholm Priory fell at the Dissolution in 1536 and has been reduced to ruins which today can only hint at the great religious house that once stood here. (*Norfolk Local Studies Library*)

Old houses, Bromholm, Bacton, *c.* 1955. This area was praised by Nikolaus Pevsner in 1962 as 'one of the prettiest in Norfolk'. With well-maintained thatched roofs, pale colour-washed walls and subtle trailing flowers, this area is still a delight to walk past or drive through. (*Author's collection*)

7

Walcott to Winterton

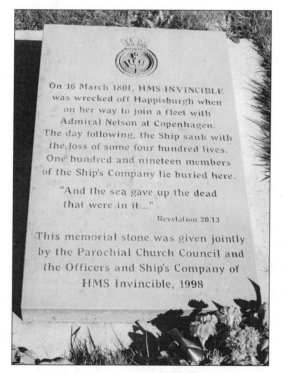

On 16 March 1801, HMS INVINCIBLE
was wrecked off Happisburgh when
on her way to join a fleet with
Admiral Nelson at Copenhagen.
The day following, the Ship sank with
the loss of some four hundred lives.
One hundred and nineteen members
of the Ship's Company lie buried here.

"And the sea gave up the dead
that were in it..."

Revelation 20:13

This memorial stone was given jointly
by the Parochial Church Council and
the Officers and Ship's Company of
HMS Invincible, 1998

Stone presented jointly by the Parochial Church
Council and Officers and Ship's Company of HMS
Invincible in 1998 in memory of the 119 members
of HMS *Invincible* buried in Happisburgh
churchyard after their ship was wrecked on the
infamous Haisbro' Sands on 16 March 1801.
(*Author's collection*)

The beach where holidaymakers rested a few months before has been gouged away dangerously close to the coast road at Walcott, December 1952. During the severe floods the following year the village was completely wrecked. A totally new sea wall and a series of defences were constructed and the shops which had been destroyed in the floods were rebuilt several hundred yards further inland. (*Author's collection*)

The reconstructed sea defences at Walcott, 1966. Another familiar feature is the line of parked cars all along the coast road here. No doubt an ice-cream van could be found crammed in somewhere along the line, selling ices and lollies to the day-trippers. (*Author's collection*)

The occupants of Manor Cottages, Walcott, flooded out after a tornado-like wind and tidal surge hit the east coast in January 1978. The sea wall was breached again and large blocks were strewn across the coast road like tumbled dice. (*Eastern Counties Newspapers*)

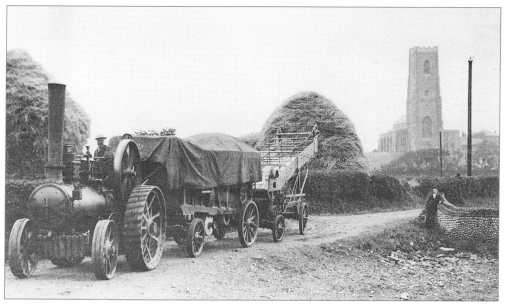

Probably one of William Gooch's threshing machines on the Walcott–Happisburgh road, *c.* 1912. Once a familiar sight rattling and hissing along the road, the traction engine, drum and elevator moved from farm to farm during harvest time. As a result of increased automation, this image was already a rare one by the 1930s. (*Author's collection*)

Church Approach, Happisburgh, *c.* 1910. The little shed to the right is Robert Amies' butcher's shop and beyond that the mighty 110ft tower of the church of St Mary. Over the years the sea has bitten away great chunks of Happisburgh and almost washed its neighbour Whimpwell away. In 1845 William White prophesied the church would be washed away by the end of the nineteenth century. She still stands firm more than 150 years later, a famous North Norfolk landmark visible from sea and land. (*Author's collection*)

The Monastery, corner of Whimpwell Street, Happisburgh, *c.* 1950. This building has features dating back to the fifteenth century. Pevsner suggested that its name might be derived from when the property belonged to Wymondham Abbey, to which William d'Albini had given the manor and church of Happisburgh in 1101. (*Author's collection*)

Whimpwell Street, Happisburgh, *c.* 1905. In 1887 the Norfolk antiquarian Walter Rye wrote rather unkindly of Happisburgh: 'There is only one general shop; no meat is to be bought except at arbitrary and erratic intervals . . . [It has] the vilest roads that I have ever come across . . . no newspaper or book has ever been seen in the village . . . and dullness reigns supreme over the district.' The quiet serenity of the village must have been missed by the great antiquarian – as my grandfather said, 'He must a' gone when the wind was a blowin'.' (*Author's collection*)

Happisburgh lighthouse having its windows cleaned, 1907. Built in 1791 and originally powered by candles, its famous red stripes were painted on in 1883 when it also had an occulting light installed. In 1942 electricity was installed. In 1987 Trinity House gave notice of closure and the old light was only saved in the nick of time by a team of locals led by Kay Swann, who formed the Happisburgh Lighthouse Trust and gained a private act of parliament and royal assent to save it. (*Author's collection*)

Lifeboat house, Happisburgh, *c.* 1910. The RNLI established a station here in 1866 and built the lifeboat house the same year for £189. Beside it is the headquarters of the Happisburgh Beach Company, complete with boards and a carved figurehead salvaged from a wreck. After the lifeboat station closed in 1926 it was used as a coastguard lookout until 1935 when a purpose-built lookout was constructed nearby. It fell into disrepair and was demolished in 1955. (*Author's collection*)

The Happisburgh lifeboat *Jacob and Rachel Valentine* being pulled into action by a ten-horse team from Love's Farm, *c.* 1909. Serving Happisburgh between 1907 and 1926, she was launched sixteen times and saved nineteen lives. (*Norfolk Local Studies Library*)

Carts and villagers await the discharge of the cargo from this barge which had run ashore at Happisburgh in April 1936. (*Author's collection*)

Canastra III, RAF Coltishall's entry in the Happisburgh to Sea Palling raft race, August 1976. Fifteen rafts took part. The previous year's winner from the Seaview Hotel, Mundesley, covered the 3½-mile course in thirty-seven minutes but because of the rule that no team could take the shield in consecutive years, the official winners were Norfolk Broads who took forty seconds longer. Second was *Wavy Liner* and RAF Coltishall were third. (*Author's collection*)

Another reminder of North Norfolk's constant battle against coastal erosion – the embattled tower of St Mary's Church, Eccles, *c.* 1890. Once a noted fishing town of over 2,000 acres, most of Eccles' houses have been swept away by the ravages of the sea. Ernest Suffling, author of *Land of the Broads*, recalled: 'On January 22nd [1895], a windy but bright day, I strolled on the beach and requiring a light for my pipe entered the old tower and obtained one. For 290 years the old tower had served as a beacon, but I little dreamed that I was the last person who should stand in its shade. The 23rd broke stormily . . . as the tide rose the tower received the full force of both sea and gale. . . . Between six and seven p.m. the tower fell but no one actually saw its fall, so great was the fury of the storm. On the 24th many persons came to see the fallen patriarch . . . [and all agreed] it seemed like standing beside a dead friend, when we gazed upon this well-known link with the past laying prostrate before us.' (*Author's collection*)

Sea Palling beach, *c.* 1912. To the right is the No. 2 lifeboat house built in 1899 at a cost of £710. Two lifeboats were kept at Palling on account of its proximity to the hazardous waters of the Haisbro' Sands. Once faster motorized lifeboats were delivered to Cromer and Caister the old Palling boats were retired in 1929 and 1930. Over the years they had saved more than 700 lives. (*Author's collection*)

Temple's Holiday Camp, Sea Palling, *c.* 1948. Bell tents and 'frontier facilities' – not exactly a vision akin to Billy Butlin's. The weather looks fine on this photo, and indeed it is very pleasant here when it is warm and sunny. The plant life hereabouts belies another story. Most of the scant number of trees and shrubs grow at an angle; their extremities have been blown so frequently landward by the North Sea winds they appear as though frozen. (*Norfolk Local Studies Library*)

The beach road, Sea Palling, *c.* 1931. On the left is the Lifeboat Inn. Built in the nineteenth century and extended in 1927, it was kept in the 1930s by Percy Sidney Feather, who was also one of the local fish dealers. Offering garage accommodation for cars and a parking ground, it was also a good place out of the wind-blown sands to leave your cycle, motorbike or car for the day for a few pennies. (*Author's collection*)

The Gap at Sea Palling is pictured just as visitors who came in about 1950 will remember it. Just about every building seen in this photograph, including the Lifeboat Inn on the right, was wrecked during the 1953 floods. (*Norfolk Local Studies Library*)

The Gap, Sea Palling, January 1963. During one of the coldest winters on record inland areas had snow throughout January and February; here the strong winds across the dunes caused a sand drift! (*Author's collection*)

The Cock Inn, Sea Palling, *c.* 1959. After the 1953 floods Lacons Ales who owned both The Cock and the nearby Lifeboat Inn had to consider whether to build a new Lifeboat or restore The Cock. A new Lifeboat was built at the brewery's expense. When the licence for The Cock came up for renewal there were tough decisions to be made. Considering the amount of money it would have taken to restore The Cock, combined with its now dangerous site on the bend of an increasingly busy road and the desire of Mr William Hamblin (its landlord for twenty-four years) to retire, it sadly had to close. (*Author's collection*)

The church and great barn (right), Waxham, *c.* 1935. The great barn was built in about 1570 by Sir Thomas Wodehouse. It is 180ft long and 35ft wide. After falling into disrepair it was beautifully restored between 1989 and 1992. The church also stood in a partially ruined state for a number of years. The nave was bricked in and used as a boatshed, the bells were removed and tower windows bricked up, which gave rise to the local saying 'As blind and deaf as Waxham Steeple.' (*Author's collection*)

Old Hall Farm, Waxham, *c.* 1935. Built in the early twelfth century, the house was shown on early records as Mockbeggar's Hall. This was home to the Inghams, Stapletons, Calthorpes and Sir William Wodehouse, one time court jester to James I. The part which stands today is just one wing of the original building. A high wall with crocketed pinnacles at the angles and a fifteenth-century gateway lead from the seaward side of the hall grounds. Today the sea beats on the dunes little more than 200 yards from this gateway; when it was first built this hall stood 12 miles inland. (*Author's collection*)

Partially submerged car at Waxham, February 1938. On the night of 13 February 1938 the sea was whipped into a frenzy by a northerly gale. Breaching the coastline, it flooded over 15 square miles of farms and marshes. (*Author's collection*)

A tractor and reaper which had been submerged by the flood simply had its magneto and points dried off and drove away under its own steam. After the February 1938 floods it took months for all the waters to subside again, leaving miles of rust-brown land and dead trees behind. In this area renowned for its barley it takes five years to bring the soil back into decent cultivation again. The value of damage to Horsey alone was estimated to be about £13,000. (*Author's collection*)

Horsey Mill, *c.* 1950. The second mill to be built on the site, this one was constructed in 1912 by Dan England, a Ludham millwright responsible for many of the mills and wind-pumps in the area. Built as a drainage mill, it did sterling work during the floods of 1938. It was struck by lightning in 1943 and an electric pump housed in a small shed next door took over its work. The old mill was left to rot. Restored in the 1960s by the County Council, it is open to the public, a familiar landmark for Broads visitors and coast-road drivers alike. (*Author's collection*)

A curious modern tourist attraction since their installation in 1992, these are two of the mills at the West Somerton Wind Farm, photographed in 1994. Each mill stands 90ft tall with 40ft blades weighing 28 tons each. The wind turbines turn sea breezes into enough electricity to power 1,700 homes. The latest mill installed on the site was opened in July 2000 and generates enough electricity for 4,000 homes. (*Author's collection*)

Bulmer House boarding house when it was kept by Mrs Alice Pratt, *c*. 1922. A warm and colourful village away from the main tourist route, Winterton was described by a commentator in the 1970s as 'A frontier village standing rather uneasily between the caravan coastline of Great Yarmouth and the empty sandhills reaching towards Happisburgh.' (*Author's collection*)

Beach Road, Winterton, March 1957. Local lads gather with their bikes in front of King's general stores (now a private residence). The bus from Yarmouth would wait a few minutes here before it spun around for its homeward journey. The big night out was a Tuesday when the young men would climb aboard Mr W.D. George's lorry for a trip to Yarmouth speedway. (*Author's collection*)

Winterton lighthouse, *c.* 1909. There was a lighthouse here from the seventeenth century. Purchased by Trinity House in 1837, the premises were rebuilt three years later; the structure of the light seen here dates from the last rebuild in 1870. In 1919 its last full-time lighthouse keeper, Mr Squibb, retired and the old light was auctioned off in January 1922 at the Star Hotel, Great Yarmouth for £1,550. It has passed through numerous hands since and all that remains today is the tower which is incorporated into a hotel complex. (*Author's collection*)

'Old Un' beachmen's headquarters and lookout, Winterton, *c.* 1890. Every good sailor knew of the dangerous waters around Winterton Ness which could claim hundreds of shipwrecks on a stormy night. Because of the number of wrecks, two beach companies were based here – 'Young Uns' and 'Old Uns' – each with their own fast yawls. They skilfully navigated the dangerous waters to save the lives of many mariners in distress, while looking for salvage at every possible opportunity. (*Norfolk Local Studies Library*)

Winterton beach, *c.* 1910. This was once a village that could proudly say it sent 200 men to the herring fishing trade, and did so generation after generation. However, by 1949 fewer than fifty men from the village were involved with the fishing industry. One old Winterton fisherman who could remember the good old days – and knew just about every old song associated with them too – was Sam Larner, who was often heard on BBC radio. Sadly he died in 1965. (*Author's collection*)

Winterton beach, January 1963. Villagers with improvised sledges collect coal from the beach. The fuel was spilt while part of the cargo of the grounded vessel *Crescence* was being unloaded. (*Author's collection*)

Banner headlines shout the nightmare of disaster and death on the cover of the *Eastern Daily Press* after the high winds and tidal surge during Saturday 31 January and Sunday 1 February 1953. (*Eastern Counties Newspapers*)

8

The 1953 Flood

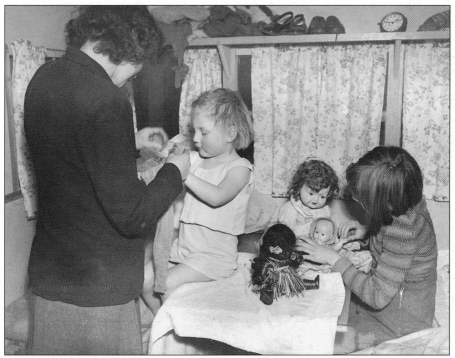

Victims of the floods, Mrs Jack Cooke and her two children Susan and Sheila, settle down into their temporary caravan home, 6 February 1953. They had been stranded in their Salthouse cottage, which had partially collapsed, until 1am on Sunday 1 February when they were able to wade to safety. (*Eastern Counties Newspapers*)

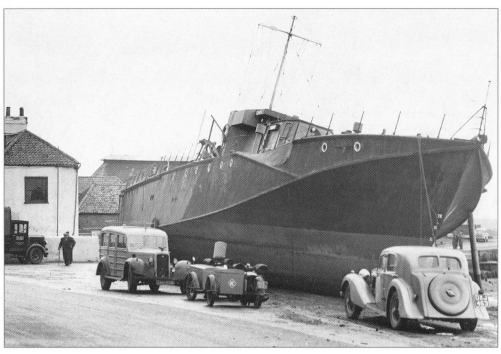

The *Terra Nova* stranded on Wells Quay, 3 February 1953. The worst flood breaches happened along the embankment from the quay to the point. Abraham's Busom was washed over and the Jubilee Café was carried away. When waters surged over the quayside the Sea Scouts Training Ship *Terra Nova* was lifted on to the quay. As the water receded it was left stranded. Its presence prevented the shops and houses behind it from being flooded. *Terra Nova* was relaunched a few weeks later by means of greased cylinders, on which it slid back into the water. It had sustained no serious damage. (*Eastern Counties Newspapers*)

Aerial view of Wells church and station taken in the week after the floods. On 31 January at about 6.30pm the tide breached the sea defences at Wells in four places. The embankment to the east of the town was broken and waters flooded the marshes up to the foot of Two Furlong Hill. In Polka Road only the glass globes on top of the petrol pumps at the garage south of the railway station were visible above the flood water. (*Eastern Counties Newspapers*)

Special visitors to the relief work at Wells, February 1953. Lady Cook (second from the right) chats with Mrs T.C. Grange at Mr N.J. Chamberlin's soup kitchen. She was one of several senior St John Ambulance staff who had been co-ordinating flood relief efforts in the county. Some of the members of the Wells St John Division who had been at the forefront of the local effort are seen on the left. (*Norfolk St John Ambulance Archive*)

Volunteers from the local fire service pumping out flooded marshes at Wells, February 1953. With extensive flooding across Slade and Church marshes they had their work cut out. Some of the waters by the quayside embankment were 15ft deep and covered an acre. (*Eastern Counties Newspapers*)

The coast road flooded at Morston, 2 February 1953. When the tidal surge came the salt marshes offered no defence against the mighty wall of water. (*Author's collection*)

With a duck for the pot and all rugged up for the foul weather, locals survey the damage and stranded boats at Blakeney. This is just one of a number of boats lifted by the tide, torn from their moorings and finally deposited along the main street and quayside when the water receded. (*Eastern Counties Newspapers*)

The engulfed coast road and wrecked houses at Salthouse. The villages of Salthouse and Cley received the full tidal force of the east coast flood. Electricity was cut out instantly, plunging the village into darkness. The swirling waters and collapsing trees greatly hampered rescue attempts led by Superintendent J.T. Briggs and Divisional Officer Elsden of Holt St John Ambulance, who had brought an ambulance and rescue crew to the scene. For their bravery, particularly in the rescue of Susan and Pamela Lascalles, they were awarded the Queen's Commendation for Gallantry and British Empire Medal respectively. (*Norfolk Local Studies Library*)

In a scene reminiscent of wartime devastation, these are the houses along the coast road at Salthouse in the aftermath of the flood on 6 February 1953. In total thirty-three properties were totally destroyed. Miraculously only one person died here; a lady who tried to escape the waters by standing on a table was swept away through her own back door. (*Eastern Counties Newspapers*)

Desperate and practical measures are seen here as a Red Cross nurse rows up Mackrell's Hill, Cley, to attend welfare cases. (*Eastern Counties Newspapers*)

Tarmac and concrete were pulverized by the force of the water along the promenade at Cromer. The chalets behind had most of their windows and interior fittings smashed and their doors were carried away by the tide. At a special Urban District Council meeting Mr R.W. Graveling said he was worried that if word of the situation got about it might have a serious effect on summer holiday bookings. (*Eastern Counties Newspapers*)

Wrecked houses at Mundesley. Locals banded together in an attempt to salvage a few items when the waters subsided. (*Author's collection*)

By far the worst hit of all the North Norfolk coastal towns and villages was Sea Palling. The sea burst through the dunes, engulfing most of the houses at the seaward end of the village. When the waters receded sand covered the village street and lay in drifts up to 5ft deep. Seven people died here. (*Author's collection*)

Dr F. Lincoln Ralphs, Norfolk's Emergency Meals Officer, with two of the soldiers drafted in to deal with the civil emergency, opening tins of soup concentrates for those who had lost their homes at Sea Palling, 8 February 1953. (*Eastern Counties Newspapers*)

Struggling to fill the gap in the dunes at Sea Palling on the third day after the flood. The fight was on to build up the defences before the next high tide; troops filled sandbags on the spot and National Servicemen and volunteers from all over Britain came to help. (*Eastern Counties Newspapers*)

Rebuilding flood-damaged houses at Salthouse, September 1953. After a vast rescue, reconstitution and welfare effort to assist those whose homes had been destroyed, the task of rebuilding the bricks and mortar of coastal communities was in full swing within a few months. Along the east coast over 32,000 people had been evacuated, and 307 people had drowned along with thousands of farm animals and domestic pets. The people who lived through those times will never forget them. The 1953 tidal surge has earned a place in history as the most catastrophic natural disaster to hit Britain in modern times. (*Norfolk Local Studies Library*)

Members of the River Board inspecting the repairs and remaining flood damage at Salthouse, May 1955. Behind them is Randall's Folly built by Onesiphorous Randall in the mid-nineteenth century. After his death in 1873 it was used by the Coastguard Service and became known as 'The Rocket House' after the rescue appliance kept there. After the First World War it was sold as a private house, and was briefly a military lookout during the Second World War. The floods caused such damage to the building that it had to be demolished and this fascinating landmark was lost forever. (*Author's collection*)

ACKNOWLEDGEMENTS

I wish to extend a very real thank you to the following without whose years of research and knowledge so generously shared with me this book would not be so enriched: Peter Brooks, Peter Cox, Ronnie Pestell and Roger Wiltshire. For additional help and the loan of photographs: Christine Swettenham and all my friends at the Muckleburgh Collection, Peter Eastell, Reg Grimes, Peter Stibbons, Steve Allen from the North Norfolk Railway and Jonathan Emery at the Sheringham Little Theatre. And last but by no means least my sincerest thanks are extended to all the library staff at Eastern Counties Newspapers and the Norfolk Local Studies Library for their generosity. Without their help this book would not have been possible.

Finally, a great thanks is due to my family for their support and love for this temperamental author.

Every attempt has been made to contact copyright holders of the images reproduced in this book. If there are any omissions in my acknowledgements, please forgive me.

The author's son Lawrence walking back across the pebbles after a paddle at Mundesley, 1999. (*Author's collection*)